Contract Management

Steven M. Bragg

AccountingTools®

ISBN 978-1-64221-156-6

Table of Contents

About the Author

Steven Bragg, CPA, has been the chief financial officer or controller of four companies, as well as a consulting manager at Ernst & Young. He received a master's degree in finance from Bentley College, an MBA from Babson College, and a Bachelor's degree in Economics from the University of Maine. He has been a two-time president of the Colorado Mountain Club, and is an avid alpine skier, mountain biker, and certified master diver. Mr. Bragg resides in Centennial, Colorado. He has written more than 300 books and courses, including *New Controller Guidebook*, *GAAP Guidebook*, and *Payroll Management*.

Steven maintains the accountingtools.com web site, which contains continuing professional education courses, the Accounting Best Practices podcast, and thousands of articles on accounting subjects.

Buy Additional AccountingTools Courses

AccountingTools offers more than 1,500 hours of CPE courses, with concentrations in accounting, auditing, finance, taxation, and ethics. Related courses that you might like include:

- Construction Accounting
- Project Management
- Purchasing Guidebook

Go to accountingtools.com/cpe to view these additional courses.

AccountingTools

Chapter 1
Contract Law

Introduction

Contracts are a key concept in business, so we have set aside a chapter to address their essential elements. This includes such matters as contract contents, the ability of a party to enter into a contract, breaches of contract, and the assignment of rights. One must have a solid foundation in these concepts in order to mitigate the litigation that sometimes accompanies contracts that are not settled to the satisfaction of all parties.

Sources of Contract Law

There are two primary sources of contract law. One is the *Uniform Commercial Code* (UCC), which is a legal code that applies to commercial transactions. The UCC was formulated in 1952 and has now been ratified by nearly all of the state governments of the United States. Some provisions of the UCC have been adopted by every state, thereby harmonizing laws pertaining to commercial transactions across the country. The Code is divided into nine articles, which cover (1) general provisions, (2) sales and leases, (3) negotiable instruments, (4) bank deposits, collections, and fund transfers, (5) letters of credit, (6) bulk transfers and bulk sales, (7) warehouse receipts, bills of lading, and other documents of title, (8) investment securities, and (9) secured transactions. Among the most important contract law in the UCC is Article 2, which covers sales and leases.

Another source of contract law is the common law of contracts, which is compiled from court decisions that have subsequently become established precedent. Most of these precedents are derived from state court decisions, with only a limited number of decisions coming from the federal courts. The provisions of the UCC generally take precedence over the common law of contracts.

The Nature of Contracts

A *contract* is an agreement between two parties that creates mutual legal obligations. It does not have to be written, but oral contracts are not recommended, since it is more difficult to legally enforce an oral contract. A valid contract must contain the following elements:

- An offer and an acceptance of that offer
- A promise to perform
- A valuable consideration
- A time or an event by which the performance must be completed
- Terms and conditions for the stipulated performance
- The actual performance

For example, a buyer offers to pay a seller of widgets $500 for the delivery of 40 widgets with a double coating of green paint, as long as they are delivered by March 15 to the buyer's facility. As an example of an alternative scenario, Mary pays Albert $10,000 not to sell his farmland to a property developer during the following one-year period; in this case, the performance is negative, since Albert is being paid *not* to do something.

The existence of a contract is decided in part by examining whether a reasonable person would conclude that the parties to it intended to enter into a contractual arrangement. For example, "I will renovate your bathroom for $15,000" sounds like a contract offer, whereas "are you interested in selling that plot of land?" does not. In the latter case, the statement made is no more than an invitation to negotiate, rather than a contract.

Offer

The formation of a contract begins with one party making an offer to another party. This is usually the result of negotiations back and forth, after which one person (the offeror) makes an offer to the other party (the offeree). This offer states the terms under which the offeror is willing to enter into a contract with the offeree. The offer is not considered effective until it is received by the offeree.

The terms of the offer must be sufficiently clear that the offeree can decide whether to accept it. For this to be the case, the offer must identify the parties, the subject matter, the quantity and price, the time of performance, and the amount to be paid. If any of these terms are indefinite, a court can insert a missing term, as long as the term is implied in the contract. For example, a price can be implied when there is an active market from which it can be derived. It is also possible to imply the time of performance. However, it is not usually possible to imply the subject matter of a contract when the item is unique, such as the design and construction of a patio for a homeowner.

There are a few special situations involving certain types of offers, which are noted in the following bullet points:

- *Advertisements.* An advertisement is legally considered to be an invitation to make an offer, which protects the seller from breach of contract suits if it runs out of the product being sold. For example, the Crumb Cake Café offers $1 off the regular price on its crumb cakes, but is not liable for breach of contract once the crumb cakes are sold out.
- *Auctions.* An auction is generally considered to be an auction with reserve, which allows the seller to refuse all bids and withdraw the goods from sale. For example, a seller offers a classic car at auction at a minimum reserve price of $250,000. The highest bid is $240,000, so the seller elects not to accept the bid. If an auctioned item is instead specifically offered without reserve, then the seller must accept the highest bid.
- *Rewards.* When the offer of a reward is made, an offeree can only collect the reward if he or she already knows about the offer when performing the requested activity. Thus, if Mr. Jones offers a $1,000 reward for information

about a warehouse break-in, and an office worker provides useful information, she can only claim the reward if she knew about it prior to providing the information.

Offer Terminations

There are several ways in which an offer can be terminated. One method is for the offeror to withdraw the offer at any time prior to when the offeree accepts it. This approach is effective as soon as the offeree receives it. Alternatively, if the offer was made to the general public, such as a reward for the return of missing goods, then it can be revoked by issuing a notice to the public via the same transmission method. Another approach to offer termination is for the offeree to reject it. Once this rejection notice has been received by the offeror, the offeree cannot subsequently accept the offer. Instead, a new offer must be made and accepted. For example, Sarah offers to sell 500 network routers to a customer for $200 each. The purchasing agent for the customer calls back and rejects the offer.

When the offeree makes a counteroffer to an offer, doing so cancels the original offer and replaces it with the counteroffer. This arrangement switches the roles of the participants, so that the offeror now becomes the offeree, and vice versa. For example, a sales manager offers to sell 1,000 widgets to a customer for $4.75 each. The customer counteroffers with a price of $4.50. The counteroffer cancels the original offer and replaces it with the $4.50 offer.

Here are several additional scenarios in which an offer can be terminated:

- When a subsequent statute renders the object of the offer illegal.
- When either the offeror or the offeree dies. The offer terminates immediately upon the death of either party.
- When the goods to be sold are destroyed, such as when the structural integrity of a building is destroyed by an earthquake.
- When the time period specified in the offer expires.

Offer Acceptance

An offer can only be validly accepted in an unequivocal manner. This means that a statement of acceptance can have only one possible meaning, without any exceptions or conditions. For example, Angie offers to sell her road bike to Victoria for $1,000, to which the response is "I think I'd like to buy it, but let me think about it." This response constitutes hedging, and so cannot be construed as an acceptance.

> **Note:** As long as an emailed acceptance to an offer has been made in an unequivocal manner, it is a valid acceptance of the offer.

An offer is only considered to have been accepted when the offeree accepts it without any attempt to modify the offer. When a modification is proposed, this constitutes a counteroffer, and so cancels the original offer. For example, a machine tool manufacturer offers to sell a lathe for $5,000, which the offeree accepts under the provision that the manufacturer include a five-year warranty. The demand for a warranty creates a counteroffer, and so voids the original offer.

An offer is not assumed to have been accepted when the offeree does not respond. This keeps an offeree from being held liable through inaction. For example, an offer to sell the offeree a car for $35,000 by Saturday unless the offeror hears otherwise does not constitute a valid acceptance. However, there are cases in which silence *is* assumed to be an offer. For example, an offeree enters into an arrangement where the same filters are sent for its air filtration units on a scheduled basis, without any formal acceptance by the offeree of each individual shipment.

An offer is assumed to have been accepted when the offeree issues an acceptance by an authorized mode of communication, even if the acceptance is then lost in transmission. This *mailbox rule* can be altered by changing the terms of an offer to state that acceptance occurs when the offeror receives the acceptance.

A final issue in regard to offer acceptance is that it must have been properly dispatched to the offeror. This means that it must have been sent to the correct address, inserted into an appropriate package, and been correctly paid for. If this has not occurred, then acceptance is not considered to have occurred until the offeror receives it. Also, if the offer stipulates that acceptance must be by a specific means of communication (such as registered mail), then an acceptance issued by any other means of communication (such as email) is not considered a valid acceptance of the offer.

Consideration

A contract is only enforceable when it involves *consideration*, which is something of legal value that is given in exchange for a promise. For example, consideration can involve the payment of cash, the transfer of property, or the promise not to engage in some type of action. Consideration has been given when (for example) one party pays another party $10,000 to forbear from engaging in a lawsuit (which involves the payment of cash in exchange for a promise not to do something).

There are several variations on the concept of consideration, which are dealt with in the following bullet points:

- *Gifts*. A promise to gift something is unenforceable, because no consideration is being given in exchange. For example, a company promises to support the local softball team with $1,000, and then refuses to issue the payment. The softball team cannot recover the money, because no consideration was offered in exchange.
- *Illegal consideration*. An offer that involves illegal consideration is not legally enforceable. For example, the owner of a small business makes $1,000 monthly payments to the local gang in exchange for their promise not to damage his shop. Their promise involves an illegal activity, and so the arrangement is void.
- *Preexisting duty*. When the party to an existing contract wants to change the terms of the deal, the proposed change is not enforceable, because the party already has an obligation to perform. For example, Joe contracted to repave a

parking lot for $150,000, and seeks to change the amount to $200,000 partway through the project. Joe already has a duty to perform for the originally-agreed amount, so the proposed change cannot be enforced.

- *Past performance.* When one party promises to pay another party based on their past performance, this promise cannot be enforced. For example, the president of a small start-up company promises an extra $20,000 to an employee for his past performance when his pay was well below the median for his job. If the president then chooses not to pay, the employee cannot enforce the payment, because the consideration was based on past performance.

Accord and Satisfaction

There are cases in which a party to a contract is dissatisfied, and wants to pay less consideration than was stated in a contract. If the parties agree to a compromise solution, this is called an *accord*. If the parties perform in accordance with the accord, this is called a *satisfaction*. Thus, the entire process is called an accord and satisfaction. If an accord is not satisfied, then the other party to the agreement can sue to enforce it.

EXAMPLE

A small mapping company enters into an arrangement with a large geographical information systems (GIS) company to license the GIS firm's database for resale, including a fixed $15,000 monthly payment for the five-year duration of the deal. It soon becomes apparent that the smaller firm cannot sell the database in sufficient quantities to pay the monthly fee, so the parties reach an accord to eliminate the fee and just pay the GIS firm an increased royalty rate on the product sales.

Promissory Estoppel

Promissory estoppel is the legal principle that a contract is enforceable, even if made without formal consideration when the offeror has made a promise to an offeree, who then relies on that promise to his or her subsequent detriment. To successfully seek a judgment under this principle, the plaintiff must prove all of the following:

- That the promisor made a promise;
- That the promisor should have expected the other party to rely upon that promise;
- That the promisee did in fact rely upon that promise; and
- It would be unjust not to enforce the promise.

EXAMPLE

The president of Medusa Medical (maker of snake oil therapies) makes an oral promise to an older employee to pay him a specific monthly amount for the duration of his upcoming retirement. The employee then retires early based on this promise, resulting in lower monthly social security payments. Medusa Medical can be legally estopped from not delivering on the promise to make the specified retirement payments, since it would harm the employee not to do so.

Contract Contents

A *covenant* is an absolute promise to perform. Therefore, not performing a covenant is a breach of contract, which allows the other party to sue. Most contract provisions are covenants.

EXAMPLE

Grouch Electronics enters into a contract to sell Michael a home entertainment system and install it in his house for $8,000. The covenants are that Grouch deliver the equipment and install it, while Michael must pay $8,000. If any of these covenants are broken, the other party can sue for nonperformance.

Many other contract provisions that are *not* covenants are various types of conditions, as noted in the following bullet points:

- *Conditions precedent*. There is a duty to perform only after there is a triggering condition. If there is no triggering condition, then there is no duty to perform. For example, an acquirer is required to pay the shareholders of the acquiree 100,000 additional shares only if the acquirer's stock price drops below $10/share.
- *Concurrent conditions*. This is a situation in which both parties agree to render the stipulated performance at the same time. For example, the delivery of 100 tomatoes to a restaurant is to be matched by payment upon their receipt.
- *Conditions subsequent*. This is a condition that excuses the other party from performance. For example, a mowing contract states that the mowing service will not mow lawns unless it has rained within the past week.

One type of condition precedent is based on satisfaction, where the recipient of services only pays for services if the level of service provided is to the satisfaction of the recipient. Legally, there are two ways to prove that satisfaction has been achieved. One is the *personal satisfaction test*, where the person given the right to reject services does so in good faith.

EXAMPLE

Douglas enters into a contract to have a painter create a landscape painting for his study; under the terms of the contract, he can reject the painting unless he is personally satisfied with the outcome.

The other test is the *reasonable person test*, which is used to evaluate most commercial contracts. As the name implies, performance by a reasonable person constitutes acceptance of performance.

EXAMPLE

Treadway Corporation, maker of paving stones and provider of related installation services, hires a software company to develop a sales tool that can assist its sales staff in designing paving installations for its customers. The provider does so, delivering a product that meets all of the criteria set forth by Treadway. Treadway's sales manager rejects the software on the grounds that he is not personally satisfied with it. This rejection constitutes a breach of contract, since the personal satisfaction test does not apply to this type of contract. Instead, application of the reasonable person test indicates that the software should have been accepted.

A "time is of the essence" clause may be inserted into a contract, stating that it has been breached if performance is not completed by the due date.

EXAMPLE

The Breckenridge Ice Festival contracts with a local ice manufacturer to deliver 20 tons of ice to the festival, to be delivered on February 4. A "time is of the essence" clause is inserted into the contract, since competing ice sculptors will need to start working on the ice as soon as it is delivered. The ice manufacturer cannot make the delivery until three days later, and so is in breach of the contract.

Proper Assent to a Contract

A contract is only valid if both parties to it voluntarily give their assent. This may not be the case in the situations described in the following sub-sections.

Duress

When a party to a contract agrees to it under duress, the person's assent is not considered to be voluntary, so the contract is not enforceable.

EXAMPLE

Doug threatens to expose Fred's relationship with a mistress to Fred's wife unless Fred agrees to sell his truck to Doug for a price well below the market rate. This constitutes the use of extortion to acquire an asset, so the contract cannot be enforced.

Fraud

A contract is void if one of the parties to it engages in fraud. *Fraud* is a false representation of the facts, resulting in the object of the fraud receiving an injury by acting upon the misrepresented facts. Thus, when one party to a contract misleads the other party through a fraudulent misrepresentation, the other party's consent to the contract is not real, so it can be voided. To prove fraud, the plaintiff must prove all of the following:

- There was a false statement of a material fact;
- The perpetrator knew that the statement was untrue;
- There was intent by the perpetrator to deceive the plaintiff;
- The plaintiff relied on the statement; and
- The plaintiff sustained an injury as a result of the preceding actions.

Though a successful plaintiff can rescind a contract and recover damages from the other party, it is entirely possible that the funds have been shifted or the perpetrator cannot be found. Consequently, the best defense against fraud is to adopt a suspicious attitude toward the statements made by others.

EXAMPLE

Alice tells Arnold that she is forming a limited liability partnership to develop an artificial heart. Arnold agrees to invest $100,000. When signing the partnership paperwork, he does not realize that she has altered it to make him a general partner, rather than a limited partner. This means that he is personally liable for all debts incurred by the business. This contract is void, since Arnold was deceived as to the nature of the agreement, and so does not know what he is signing.

EXAMPLE

Manuel agrees to sell a used sports car to Oliver for $150,000. As part of the negotiations, Oliver demands to see all of the repair records for the sports car. Manuel neglects to hand over the repair documentation associated with a crash that bent the frame of the car. By not providing the required information, Manual has engaged in fraud. Oliver can elect to sue Manuel for fraud, due to the concealment of material information.

> **Note:** Innocent misrepresentation is not fraud. This occurs when a person makes a statement that he honestly believes to be true, even though that is not the case. In this case, a plaintiff cannot sue for damages, but can rescind the contract.

When the parties to a contract do not disclose all possible information to each other, this does not necessarily constitute fraud. Realistically, it is not possible for either side to disclose everything to each other. The only cases in which disclosure is required is when there is a specific government statute requiring disclosure, when a lack of information could physically harm the other party, or when there is a relationship of trust between the parties.

EXAMPLE

The government of Iowa requires that a home seller fill out a property condition disclosure form, on which the seller states whether there have been any problems with the heating, plumbing, septic, and electrical systems of the house, as well as the presence of any asbestos or lead-based paint.

Mistakes

A contract may not be valid when one or both parties have an incorrect view of some aspect of the contract. When a mistake is made by just one party to a contract, the contract is still enforceable. However, the contract will not be enforceable if doing so would be unconscionable, the other party should have known that a mistake was made, or because the mistake was caused by a clerical error.

EXAMPLE

The purchaser of a modified Porsche acquires the vehicle under the assumption that its engine has been modified to run on diesel fuel, which is not the case. This is a unilateral mistake, so the purchaser is still required to purchase the vehicle.

The situation changes if both parties to a contract have made a mistake regarding a material fact. In this situation, the contract can be rescinded, on the grounds that it does not represent the intent of either party.

EXAMPLE

One baseball card collector, Henry, agrees to sell his Aaron Quigley card to another collector, Joseph. The trouble is that there are two baseball players named Aaron Quigley, and Henry and Joseph were referring to a different Quigley when they struck the deal. Since there is a mutual mistake of a material fact, the contract is void.

A contract cannot be voided when there are differing views about the value of the object of the contract. Thus, if one party thinks an asset is of low value and the other believes it to have a substantially higher value, there are no grounds to terminate the contract.

EXAMPLE

A database company has found few buyers for one of its databases, and so sells it to a government contractor for $100,000. The contractor knows it can sell the database to the federal government for $500,000. Despite the large disparity in perceived values of the database, there are no grounds to void the contract.

Undue Influence

It is possible that one party to a contract will exercise undue influence over the other. This situation arises when one party takes advantage of the weaknesses of the other party, perhaps due to age or infirmity, to force the weaker party to enter into a disadvantageous contract. A contract will be voidable under these circumstances, as long as the plaintiff can prove that a fiduciary relationship existed between the parties, and that the other party used his or her influence to convince the other party to enter into the contract.

EXAMPLE

Mr. Smith is badly injured in a car accident, and is permanently bedridden. Prior to the accident, he executed a will in which he left all of his possessions to two daughters. His long-term insurance company then provides him with a live-in nurse, Geoffrey, who tends to him for the next year, after which he dies. Following his death, a revised will is discovered that gives a large portion of Mr. Smith's estate to Geoffrey. If the daughters can prove that Geoffrey used his dominant position to influence Mr. Smith into altering his will, then the will can be invalidated.

Ability to Enter into a Contract

There are several situations in which a contract has been held to be invalid, either because it involves an illegal activity or because one of the parties to it is not legally able to enter into it. In the following sub-sections, we note a variety of these situations.

Contracts with Minors

Many state governments have laws mandating that people must be at least 18 years old before they can enter into a contract. This is done on the grounds that minors do not have the experience or maturity to enter into contracts. Further, minors have the right to cancel most contracts that they have entered into with an adult. Conversely, an adult does not have this right when the counterparty to a contract is a minor. This right of cancellation is useful for cancelling contracts that are disadvantageous to a minor. However, a minor cannot cancel contracts for necessary items, such as shelter, food, clothing, and medical services.

A minor can cancel a contract in several ways, including through the use of a written notification, a verbal statement, or via his or her conduct.

At the point when a minor cancels a contract, the minor must return any consideration received from the adult, in the condition it is in at that time. This can mean that the value of the consideration will have declined by the time it is returned, creating a loss for the adult. However, if the loss in value was intentional or due to gross negligence by the minor, then the full value of the consideration must be returned. Full value of the consideration must also be returned when a minor misrepresents his or her age to the adult.

Conversely, an adult participating in a contract that has been cancelled must return any consideration received from the minor; if the consideration has declined in value or been sold, then the adult must return the cash equivalent of its value.

EXAMPLE

Michael is 17 years old. He enters into a contract with Albert (an adult) to buy a riding mower for $4,000. Albert does not inquire into Michael's age. Michael pays the $4,000 to Albert and receives the mower in exchange. A few months later, when Michael is still 17, a tree falls over and crushes the mower (not when he is riding it). The mower is heavily damaged, and is now worth only $1,000. Michael cancels the contract and returns the mower to Albert, who must return the full $4,000 to Michael. The end result is that Michael recovers all of the $4,000 purchase price, while Albert has a damaged mower that is only worth $1,000.

If Michael had instead misrepresented his age to Albert, then he would only have been able to recover $1,000 from Albert.

If a minor does not cancel a contract by the time he or she becomes an adult, then the contract is considered to have been accepted. This means that the former minor is now bound by the contract.

Contracts with Mentally Incompetent Individuals

When mentally incompetent people enter into a contract, they are not bound to it, on the grounds that they may not understand the consequences of the contract on them. To be released from the terms of a contract, a person must have been legally insane when he or she entered into it. Legal insanity is present when a person cannot understand the nature of a transaction.

When a court has judged a person to be insane, then any contract entered into by that person is void. Only the person's court-appointed guardian then has the authority to enter into contracts on behalf of the individual. If there has been no formal court judgment that a person is insane, but the person suffers from a mental impairment, then the individual can void any contract that he or she enters into. When the other party to a contract was not aware that a person was insane and the contract is voided, then the other party is due full restitution for any consideration given.

Contracts with Intoxicated Individuals

In most states, when people enter into contracts while intoxicated, they can declare these contracts to be void. This is only the case when a person was so intoxicated that he or she could not understand the nature of the transaction. When a contract is voided under these circumstances, consideration must be returned to the other party and restitution made to return the other party to its position before the contract.

Illegal Contracts

A contract cannot be enforced if it is illegal. This includes any contract to perform illegal activities, such as an agreement to dump toxic fluids in the local river. As another example, a loan agreement that mandates a higher interest rate than is allowed by a state's usury laws is illegal. Since an illegal contract is void, neither party to it can sue the other for nonperformance.

EXAMPLE

Sharper Designs, a maker of knives, enters into a contract to deliver 10,000 of its titanium blades to a distributor in Canada. However, the President of the United States issues an executive order, imposing sanctions on Canada and making it illegal for United States corporations to do business with Canadians (apparently due to the well-known combative nature of Canadians). Since the sales arrangement is now illegal, Sharper Designs refuses to ship the knives to the Canadian distributor.

There are a few cases in which certain aspects of an illegal contract can be enforced. For example, when someone is forced into a contract under duress, they can recover the consideration paid. As another example, when a party enters into an illegal contract, pays for the illegal performance, and then backs out before the performance occurs can sue to recover the payment.

EXAMPLE

The president of Curmudgeons International pays an employee of Killjoy & Sons $25,000 to hand over insider information about Killjoy's financial performance. The president has second thoughts about the deal and backs out before any insider information is delivered. Curmudgeons can recover the $25,000 payment.

Unconscionable Contracts

An *unconscionable contract* is so one-sided that it is unfair to one party and therefore unenforceable under the law. A contract is considered to be unconscionable when the following issues are present:

- When one party has an unreasonable advantage over the other;
- When the dominant party uses its advantage to obtain unfair contract terms; and
- When the other party had no other practical alternative than to enter into the contract.

Unconscionable contracts are most commonly found in situations where a business is taking advantage of elderly, uneducated, or poor people who do not understand the terms of the contracts being presented to them.

A court can take several approaches to dealing with unconscionable contracts. One is to refuse to enforce any part of the contract, while another option is to not enforce just those portions of the contract that it determines to be unconscionable.

EXAMPLE

A payday lender offers cash loans to low-income workers who do not have bank accounts, charging 500% interest on these loans that compounds on a weekly basis. The loan agreements also mandate that borrowers pay the entire cost of any collection activities conducted by the lender. This arrangement would certainly be considered an unconscionable contract, if only because the interest rate being charged is far beyond the maximum rate allowable under state law.

Discharge of Performance

There are several alternatives for discharging the performance obligations of the parties to a contract. One possibility is a discharge by agreement, where the parties mutually agree to cancel the contract. If only one party to an agreement cancels it, this constitutes a breach of contract. Another approach is to substitute the contract with another one that discharges the original contract. Yet another possibility is a *novation*, where a third party takes the place of one of the original parties to the contract; this is only legal if all three parties agree to the change. Another alternative is an accord and satisfaction arrangement, where the parties agree to a different arrangement to settle the obligations stated in the original contract. Completion of the terms of the alternative arrangement discharges the original contract. And a final option is discharge by impossibility, where the contract is discharged due to it being illegal, or because the promisor in a personal services contract has died, or because the subject of the contract has been destroyed. For example, a contract to sell a building is discharged by impossibility when the building is destroyed in an earthquake.

Rock Solid Sailboats enters into a contract to build a 100' concrete sailboat for a client. However, the radical design proposed for the project fails during tests of a mock-up model. In an accord and satisfaction arrangement, the two parties agree to replace the original contract with a more traditional fiberglass version of the same design. Once this replacement has been delivered to the client, Rock Solid's obligations under the original contract are discharged.

Breach of Contract

There are several thresholds used to define the extent to which a contract has been breached, which also drives the amount of damages associated with a breach. We cover these issues in the following sub-sections.

Levels of Contractual Performance

There are several levels at which a contract is considered to have been completed. The lowest level of completion is inferior performance, where there is a material contractual breach. Substantial completion represents only a minor breach of contract, while strict performance discharges all obligations.

Strict performance is the outcome of most contractual arrangements, and results when all terms stipulated in a contract have been met. For example, a contractual arrangement mandates that Colossal Furniture manufacture 10 oversized sofas and deliver them to Homestead Furniture, a distributor, in exchange for a payment of $20,000. Colossal delivers the sofas and Homestead pays the stipulated amount, so both parties have engaged in strict performance of the contract.

Substantial performance has taken place when there is only a minor breach of the terms of a contract, typically involving a minor deviation from a strict performance level. If this breach is not remediated, the other party can either pay a reduced amount to cover the cost to correct the deviation, or sue for recovery of this cost. For example, an office remodeling project requires the contractor to apply two layers of paint to the walls, but only one layer is applied. The tenant can either have someone else complete the painting for $20,000 and deduct this amount for the contractor's final billing, or sue the contractor for reimbursement of this amount.

Inferior performance occurs when the actions of a party impair or destroy the essence of a contract. Whether a party's performance can be construed as substantive performance or inferior performance depends on the circumstances of each case. When the aggrieved party alleges inferior performance, one remedy is to seek repayment of any amounts paid, as well as to cancel the contract.

EXAMPLE

A real estate developer contracts with a construction company to build an office tower in an area subject to earthquakes, with requirements to construct a building sufficiently robust to withstand substantial earthquake activity. What the contractor delivers is entirely substandard, so the developer sues for cancellation of the contract, repayment of all fees paid, and demolition of the building by the construction company.

Monetary Damages

Either minor or material breaches can be remedied with the payment of monetary damages. There are several types of monetary damages, as noted in the following bullet points:

- *Compensatory damages.* This payment compensates the plaintiff for losses suffered from nonfulfillment of a contract. For example, a power company enters into a 10-year agreement to buy natural gas from a natural gas pipeline operator, taking deliveries for $4 million per year. After six years, the power company abrogates the contract, which is a material breach. The pipeline can sue the power company for $16 million (calculated as the four remaining years on the contract, multiplied by the $4 million fee per year). However, if the pipeline company finds an alternate customer for its natural gas at the same price, then it cannot sue for compensatory damages.
- *Consequential damages.* This payment is for losses that do not flow directly and immediately from a contractual breach, but which result indirectly from it. These damages are only paid when the plaintiff can prove that the breaching party knew that its contractual breach would cause additional damages to the other party. For example, a breach of contract relating to a retail store not being completed on time results in a loss of anticipated profits from having that store operational.
- *Liquidated damages.* The amount of this payment is stipulated within a contract. Liquidated damages are enforceable when the stated amount is reasonable, and when it is difficult to determine actual damages. For example, a liquidated damages provision for $100,000 is included in a contract to design a new electric hydrofoil ship for a client. The design does not work, and the client loses several million dollars because the resulting ship must be scrapped. In this case, the client's only remedy is the $100,000 in liquidated damages stated in the contract.
- *Tort damages.* In rare cases, a plaintiff can pursue additional tort damages for pain and suffering, emotional distress, and sometimes even punitive damages. One can pursue any third party for tort damages when they intentionally interfere with a contract, causing injury to the plaintiff. For example, a well-known college professor enters into a five-year employment contract with a major university to teach there. A year later, another university with full knowledge of this contract offers the professor a large boost in pay to work

for it instead – which the professor does. In this case, the first university can recover tort damages from the second university for intentional interference with a contract.

Many businesses guard against losses related to consequential damages by inserting a disclaimer into their sales agreements, making them not responsible for these types of losses.

EXAMPLE

A museum stores rare manuscripts in a climate-controlled vault. It purchases a new humidity control system from a supplier for $20,000. The sales agreement to which the museum agreed includes a consequential damages clause. Over a weekend when no one is on the premises of the museum, the control system fails, resulting in irreparable harm to dozens of manuscripts. Because of the disclaimer, the museum will not win consequential damages in court, but can sue for compensatory damages, where it can recover the $20,000 cost of the control system.

When a plaintiff wants to sue for damages, it must make reasonable efforts to mitigate those damages. For example, if the poor performance of a roofing company causes a leak, the plaintiff must take all reasonable steps to mitigate the resulting water damage following a storm.

Alternative Approaches

There are alternative ways to deal with a contract that has been breached. One approach is *rescission*, which involves undoing a contract and having the parties return all property and money to each other. The intent is to return the parties to their original positions before entering into the contract.

EXAMPLE

Albemarle Publishers sends a $50,000 royalty advance to David Withers for his forthcoming book, *Tide of the Soldiers*, which is due in May. A year after that, the manuscript is still not complete. This is a material breach. Albemarle can rescind the contract, which means that Mr. Withers must return the advance, and he can also shop for a new publisher.

If it is not possible to adequately compensate a plaintiff with monetary damages, there are several alternatives available. One is specific performance, where the breaching party is required to complete the tasks stated in the contract. Specific performance is an option when the performance required in a contract is unique. Examples of the situations in which such performance may be required include the sale of real property, heirlooms, and collections. Personal service contracts cannot be enforced with specific performance.

EXAMPLE

Alfred and Morgan enter into a contract, under which Alfred will sell the classic "Still Life with Chevrolet" painting to Morgan for $500,000 on May 5. On May 5, Morgan arrives with the $500,000, but Alfred refuses to sell the painting to Morgan. Since this is a unique item, Morgan can bring an action for specific performance against Alfred in order to obtain a judgment ordering Alfred to sell the painting to Morgan.

Another alternative approach applies to situations in which there are clerical errors in a contract. In these cases, a court can rewrite the contract to make it conform to the actual intentions of the parties to it. For example, a contract to transfer a property is supposed to mandate the transfer on June 6 of the current year, but the person who prepared the contract set the date for two years in the future. The court can correct this error to set the date back to the current year.

A court may issue an *injunction* to prohibit an action. This is done when a party to a contract can prove that he or she will otherwise suffer an irreparable injury. Injunctions are only issued under very limited circumstances.

Contracts that Must Be in Writing

As noted in the following sub-sections, certain types of contracts must be in writing and contain specific clauses for them to be enforceable.

Basic Concepts

According to state law, several types of contracts must be in writing. This requirement is used to ensure that key contract terms are not misunderstood, and to minimize the risk of fraud. The main types of contracts that must be in writing are as follows:

- Contracts for the lease of goods involving payments of at least $1,000
- Contracts for the sale of goods valued at $500 or more
- Contracts in which one party guarantees the debt of another
- Contracts involving real property
- Contracts that cannot be completed within one year
- Contracts to pay a finder's fee
- Contracts to pay debts that have been barred by the statute of limitations or discharged
- Contracts with real estate agents

When a contract for the sale of goods is initially for less than $500 but is then increased so that the total is for a larger amount, then the modification to the original agreement must be in writing.

EXAMPLE

Herman owns an Airstream camper, which he verbally promises to sell to Alice for $40,000. However, he refuses to turn over the camper to Alice when she shows up a week later with the purchase price. Since the agreement was for more than $500 and is not is writing, it is not enforceable.

When an oral agreement intended to cover a short period of time is extended to cover a period of more than one year, it should be in writing. This can result in situations where someone promising to make payments under an oral agreement for an extended period of time can legally avoid any payments due to be paid after one year has elapsed, since the agreement should have been in writing.

EXAMPLE

The board of directors of a nonprofit entity fires its executive director, and appoints one of the firm's staff to be the temporary executive director under an oral agreement that is not expected to last more than three months. This person is so good that the board decides to hire her for an additional year. Since this extension results in a total contract duration of 15 months, it should be in writing.

When one party guarantees the debt of another, it must be in writing. This arrangement is between the guarantor and the party that is extending credit to a third party. The guarantor will only be required to pay the creditor if the original borrower fails to pay the debt. This situation commonly arises when the parents of a young adult assist that person in his or her purchase of a vehicle. The creditor will not extend credit, since the borrower does not yet have a credit history. As long as the parents agree in writing to pay if the son or daughter does not pay, the creditor will agree to grant credit.

Note: When the main point of a guarantee arrangement is to provide a benefit to the guarantor, then the agreement does not have to be in writing.

EXAMPLE

George is the sole owner of Smithy Ironworks. Smithy borrows $50,000 from the Midas Industrial Bank, and George orally guarantees that he will personally repay the debt if Smithy cannot. Midas can enforce this promise, since the loan will benefit George, as the sole shareholder.

When a contract that is required to be in writing is not, it is generally unenforceable. In cases where an oral contract that should have been in writing has already been completed, then neither party to it can rescind the contract.

The most common type of contract that must be in writing involves real property (such as the sale of land and buildings). For example, a contract to purchase a house must be in writing, as must the mortgage agreement associated with it, since the mortgage gives the lender a security interest in the property.

Contents of a Written Contract

To be legally effective, a written contract can take many forms. At its most precise, it may have been constructed by one's attorney, but a written contract can also be considered valid if it is in the form of a letter, an invoice, or even handwritten notes scribbled on some paper. In all cases, however, the following rules apply to a written contract:

- *Best evidence.* The best evidence of the terms of a contract is considered to be within the final contract. Any prior writings or verbal agreements are irrelevant to the terms of the final contract. This means that any promises made outside of a final contract will be disallowed in court. However, outside evidence may be used to clarify ambiguous wording, correct a clerical error, or fill in gaps not addressed in the final contract (such as a missing price).
- *Incorporation by reference.* A contract can include other documents that are referenced in the main document. This can result in a substantial contract, even though the main document is quite short. Incorporation by reference can include physically attaching documents together, such as with a staple or paper clip.
- *Ranking of text.* When the parties employ a preprinted form contract, words typed into the contract are given precedence over the preprinted text. Also, handwritten text is given precedence over both preprinted and typed text.
- *Resolution of ambiguity.* When a clause within a contract is ambiguous, a court will resolve it against the party that wrote the contract.
- *Signature.* The contract must be signed by the party who may be the subject of an enforcement action. This means that a contract may only have one signer. A signature can appear anywhere on a document, and does not need to be the individual's full legal name.

Assignment of Rights

The parties to a contract may be able to transfer their contractual rights to other parties, which is called an *assignment of rights.*

EXAMPLE

Absolution Corporation sells supplies to several thousand churches, usually under 30-day payment terms. Absolution suddenly finds itself short of cash, and so sells $250,000 of its accounts receivable to a third party in exchange for the immediate payment of cash, less a 3% discount. In this case, Absolution has assigned its right to collect the accounts receivable to a third party.

Several special situations apply to the assignment of rights. Consider the following:

- *Breach of contract.* The rights relating to a breach of contract can be assigned. For example, a credit card company assigns its right to collect a number of overdue account balances to a collection agency in exchange for a cash payment.
- *Multiple assignments.* An assignor may fraudulently assign a contractual right to more than one party. If so, the first assignee will prevail in court, where the date and time of the assignment is the deciding factor. For example, a financially troubled company sells its receivables to Seth for $80,000, and again the next day to Mary, for $75,000. Since Seth was assigned the receivables first, he obtains the right to collect the receivables over Mary. Mary must sue the assignor to recover her payment.
- *Notice of assignment.* When the rights under a contract have been assigned to a third party, the party to which the rights were assigned must notify the obligor (the party with an obligation to perform) of the assignment. For example, when the right to collect a loan has been sold, the assignee must notify the borrower that all payments must now be sent to the assignee. If the assignee does not provide this notice, then the assignee can only collect from the assignor any payments subsequently paid out by the borrower to the assignor.
- *Personal services.* A contract for the delivery of personal services cannot be assigned, except in cases where assignment is specifically allowed. For example, when a singer signs a contract to perform at a specific arena, that contract cannot be assigned to a different venue.
- *Right to delegate.* The obligation to perform duties can usually be delegated to a third party, unless a contract states otherwise. The delegating party is the delegator, and the entity to which this responsibility is delegated is the delegatee. For example, a city ordinance requires that a home have a smoke detector in each bedroom. The homeowner delegates this responsibility to an electrician.

Special Business Arrangements

In the following sub-sections, we address the contractual implications of several special business arrangements.

Contracts in Restraint of Trade

Restraint of trade is any activity that prevents another party from conducting business as they normally would without such restraint. For example, two companies agreeing to fix prices in order to impede the business of a competitor is an illegal restraint of trade. Another classic example of restraint of trade is when several businesses merge in order to form a monopoly.

EXAMPLE

Cantilever Construction and Truss Corporation agree to fix the prices of their bids for various bridge design and construction contracts, so that they can keep prices high. Since this arrangement is in restraint of trade, any contracts resulting from it are void, and so cannot be enforced by either party to it.

Not all contracts in restraint of trade are illegal. For example, the purchaser of a business could require the former owners to enter into a non-compete agreement as a condition of the sale, as long as the terms of the agreement are reasonable (such as only having a term of a few years). Employers may also require key employees to sign non-compete agreements as part of their employment contracts. These agreements are held to be valid as long as they are reasonable in regard to the scope of the line of business and geographic area being protected, as well as the duration of the restriction.

EXAMPLE

Melvin sells his dentistry practice in Pueblo, Colorado to Andrew. As part of the sale agreement, Melvin agrees not to open another dentistry practice anywhere in Colorado for the next 15 years. This non-compete agreement is reasonable in regard to the line of business being protected (dentistry), but not in regard to the geographic area (an entire state) or the duration (15 years). If the agreement had instead only limited Melvin to opening another practice within the same city and within the next few years, it would have been entirely enforceable.

Impact of Licensing Arrangements

When a state government imposes a licensing statute on certain professions, it is requiring people to be licensed in order to do business within those professions. Licensing applies to many professions, including auditors, lawyers, doctors, and teachers. This requirement is imposed in order to maintain certain minimum standards within each profession. Some states do not give unlicensed persons the right to enforce contracts relating to these service areas.

EXAMPLE

Philip has a degree in accounting but has failed the CPA examination, and so is not a licensed CPA. He agrees to conduct an audit for a small local contractor that needs the audit in order to obtain a bank loan, in exchange for a $7,500 fee. Since he is not a licensed CPA, Phil cannot enforce the contract and recover the payment from the contractor.

Exculpatory Clauses

An *exculpatory clause* is a contract provision that relieves one party of liability if damages occur during the execution of a contract. The party that inserts the clause is probably the one seeking to be relieved of the potential liability. For example, a ski

21

resort prints an exculpatory clause on its ski passes, stating that it is not responsible for injuries suffered by skiers on the ski resort's property. These clauses are usually enforceable, since they typically are included in arrangements where the other party is voluntarily participating in an activity that has some degree of risk associated with it.

Exculpatory clauses are not valid when they are designed to relieve a party from acts of gross negligence, fraud, or reckless behavior. They may also be voided if they have a significant impact on the public interest.

Types of Contracts

There are several types of contracts, each with different characteristics. The primary contract types are as follows:

- *Bilateral contract*. This is a contract in which both parties exchange promises to perform. An example is when Hammer Industries offers to purchase a backhoe from Franklin Construction for $65,000, to which Franklin agrees. Hammer can then sue if the backhoe is not delivered, and Franklin can sue if Hammer does not pay for it.
- *Unilateral contract*. This is a contract in which an offeror promises to pay after the occurrence of a specified act. There is no contract until the act occurs. A unilateral contract cannot be revoked by the offeror once the offeree has begun work. An example is when a homeowner offers Maid Marian (a cleaning service) $250 if it can clean her house by March 15. Only if Maid Marian cleans the house by March 15 does the homeowner owe the $250 to the company. At this point, Maid Marian would be able to sue to collect payment of the $250.
- *Formal contract*. This is a contract that is in conformance with any requirements and standards, and is legally binding and enforceable. An example is a check, which is created in a special form, and which must use certain language stated in the UCC.
- *Informal contract*. This is any sort of contract entered into that does not require any particular method or form. These contracts are enforceable. An example is an agreement between a homeowner and a lawn mowing service, for the service to mow the homeowner's lawn at regular intervals.
- *Express contract*. This is a contract whose terms the parties have explicitly set out. Most contracts are classified as express contracts. An example is a written agreement to sell land to a business, including all real property located on it.
- *Implied contract*. This contract is created when several parties have no written contract, but one can be inferred from their conduct. Such a contract can be inferred when one party provides property or services to the other party in expectation of payment, and the other party has the opportunity to reject what is provided. An example is when a budding songwriter discusses lyrics with an advertising agency, which does not offer to pay her a royalty. The agency

then derives an ad jingle that is substantially similar to the lyrics she presented to it. The songwriter can claim that an implied contract was in place, and recover damages from the ad agency.

- *Quasi contract.* This is a situation in which one party is judged to have an obligation to another party, even in the absence of a formal contract. This condition is considered to be present when one party has been given goods or services with the expectation of being paid, they have been accepted, and the other party will be unjustly enriched unless the court requires payment based on the reasonable value of the goods or services received. An example is when a steer owned by a rancher is about to die from a rare disease; a passing veterinarian diagnoses the problem, saves the steer, and then sends the rancher a bill for services performed. The rancher has an obligation to pay the bill.
- *Output contract.* This is a contract in which the seller agrees to sell all of its output to just one buyer. This arrangement assures the seller of having a firm buyer, while assuring the buyer of a reliable source. An example is when a molybdenum mine agrees to sell all of its output to a steel mill, which uses it as an alloying agent in the production of steel.
- *Requirements contract.* The flip side of the preceding output contract is a requirements contract, in which a buyer commits to buy all of its requirements for a specific item from just one seller. This benefits the buyer by assuring it of a firm source, while the seller eliminates all associated selling costs. An example is a furniture manufacturer that sources all of its wood from one lumber mill. Under this arrangement, the lumber mill can still sell any of its remaining output to other parties.

An additional issue that relates to the performance associated with a contract is the *executory contract.* This is a contract that has not yet been fully performed or fully executed. It is a contract in which both sides still have important performance remaining. Once both sides have fully performed, the contract is then known as an executed contract. For example, Prickly Corporation has entered into an agreement to ship $5,000 of thornbushes to an arboretum. It has not yet shipped the thornbushes, and the arboretum has not paid for them, so this is an executory contract.

Plain-Language Contracts

Many contracts are poorly structured, and full of unnecessary and incomprehensive language. For example, is it really necessary to sprinkle a legal document with such phrases as "subject to the foregoing" and "notwithstanding anything to the contrary herein"? Instead, contracts should be structured to be readable by someone who has not earned a law degree. Restructuring contracts to make them more readable has several advantages, including reducing their length, reducing the time required to negotiate them, and minimizing the number of changes made by the opposing party.

Ideally, a contract should be written so that it can be easily understood by someone with a high school education, and with no knowledge of the context within which the contract was written. Doing so requires that a contract be revised with input from the departments impacted by the contract, rather than just the legal department. Thus, contracts relating to the sale of products to a customer should certainly include input from the sales department, and possibly also the engineering and customer support departments. These parties should be able to provide the legal staff with a solid grounding in the actual risks associated with a business arrangement, so that the attorneys can craft a contract that only deals with these risks – thereby avoiding any boilerplate risk management clauses that are essentially useless for the situations covered by a contract.

A few principles to follow when devising plain-language contracts are as follows:

- Keep sentences short
- Use the active voice
- Eliminate all definitions

The ultimate metric of whether a contract has been properly written in plain language is that it should reduce the amount of contract negotiation time with counterparties. When this is not the case, then revise the clauses for which counterparties want to make changes in order to clarify their meaning.

Summary

Not having a well-founded knowledge of contracts can result in a business being caught off-guard when it is judged to be liable for a contract that was not completed to the satisfaction of a plaintiff. The subjects covered in this chapter reduce the risk of this happening, since a contract manager can now be forewarned about such matters as when a contract has to be in writing, what constitutes a breach of contract, and when performance is considered to be discharged.

Chapter 2
Contract Terms and Conditions

Introduction

Contracts define the terms and conditions under which two entities agree to do business with each other. The intent of a contract is for both organizations to engage in activities that are beneficial to them. However, a poorly-designed or incorrectly managed contract can result in acrimonious relations, so it makes sense to be aware of the implications of every clause in a contract, as well as how contracts should be monitored on an ongoing basis. In this chapter, we cover contract terms and conditions, contract pricing arrangements, and several related matters.

Contract Terms and Conditions

The terms and conditions included in a contract define the rules for how a contract is to be administered. Terms and conditions typically include the following subjects:

Header

- *Date*. States the date of the contract. This can be of some importance, if the contract spans a certain number of days. Setting the date back can reduce the effective span of a contract.
- *Parties*. States the legal names of the entities entering into the contract, along with their addresses. Can be important if only the name of a subsidiary is used, since it reduces the legal liability of the parent entity.

Terms and Conditions

- *Definitions*. There will be many terms in each contract; they are defined at the beginning of the contract, where all parties can easily reference them. Definitions can be surprisingly useful since even a common term may be mis-interpreted. For example, it may be necessary to define the word "price," because it could refer to just the base price of an item, or it may also include discounts, sales taxes, rush charges, freight, and so forth.
- *Acceptance criteria*. This clause notes the criteria that will be applied when the buyer examines the supplier's deliveries. The criteria can be quite detailed, and so may be expanded upon in an accompanying schedule.
- *Confidentiality*. This clause notes that all information shared by the parties is not to be shared with other parties. This is of most concern when a buyer is sending intellectual property to a supplier, and does not want a competitor to see it, or to have information leaked to the public.

- *Currency*. This clause states the currency in which payments will be made. This can be a useful way to avoid foreign currency risk, by forcing the supplier to accept payment in the buyer's home currency.
- *Cyber security*. This clause requires that all work related to the contract be subject to the buyer's cyber security requirements.
- *Delay notifications*. This clause requires the seller to promptly notify the buyer when conditions arise that will delay a deliverable or increase its cost, noting the details of the delay, its expected extent, and its specific impact. The lack of a timely notification prevents the seller from billing the buyer for incremental increases in the associated cost.
- *Dispute resolution*. This clause mandates that a sequence of actions be taken to resolve disputes between the parties. This begins with attempts at resolution by the respective project managers, which then escalates to the managers of the respective parties. If a satisfactory conclusion cannot be reached, the parties are required to accept arbitration, thereby avoiding the expense and delay associated with using the court system. Alternatively, there may be a clause mandating the prior use of mediation before taking a dispute into the court system. See the Contractual Disputes section for more information.
- *Effective dates*. This clause states the start and ending dates of the agreement. An issue in this clause is any automatic extension, stating that the contract will automatically renew unless proper notice is given by one party to the other. This can be a contract management issue, involving monitoring the contract termination date well in advance.
- *Force majeure*. This clause identifies those events that are considered outside of the control of the parties, such as wars, embargos, riots, sabotage, acts of terrorism, hurricanes, fires, and floods. When any of these events arise, the performing party may be absolved from performance entirely, or is given a reasonable extension of time in which to perform its obligations. When claiming force majeure, the performing party must use reasonable efforts to minimize the effects of any delay.

Note: Force majeure events do not include strikes, work stoppages, labor disputes, or the late delivery of materials or equipment.

- *Governing law*. This is a designation of the court of law in which any disputes between the parties will be settled. The buyer usually wants the court to be located nearby, to reduce its travel costs. If both parties are located close to each other, then this clause is a minor one.
- *Insurance*. The buyer may not want any supplier liabilities to spill over onto it, and so will be quite specific about the types and amounts of insurance that it wants a supplier to maintain. This clause may also state that a supplier forward certificates of insurance to the buyer, proving that the mandated insurance is currently valid. A large buyer can force these terms onto a smaller

supplier, but this can be a more contentious issue when the bargaining positions of the parties are more even.

- *Intellectual property.* A potentially major issue is which of the parties owns any intellectual property that arises from work performed under a contract. The buyer usually wants to take ownership of any intellectual property created, so that a supplier cannot sell it to a competitor. If the rights are split, this clause needs to specify the nature of the split rights. This clause is much less of a concern when commodity-grade goods are being purchased, since there should be no associated intellectual property.

- *Liabilities.* The buyer typically uses this clause to make the supplier responsible for any losses and liabilities arising from the contract. The supplier will probably want to limit its liability to the replacement of the goods being sold to the buyer. The buyer may attempt to expand the liability to include lost profits or other damages or injuries caused by the supplier's goods or services; this presents a much greater liability for the supplier. Several variations on the range of liabilities are:

  o *Actual damages.* These are the actual losses incurred by the buyer within the range of circumstances defined within a contract.
  o *Consequential damages.* These are losses arising as a consequence of the actions of a party to a contract.
  o *Cover damages.* This is the incremental additional cost incurred by the injured party to replace goods that should have been provided by the other party.
  o *Incidental damages.* This is essentially reimbursement for the incidental expenses incurred by the damaged party to cover for the breach of contract by the other party.
  o *Liquidated damages.* This is a predetermined amount to be paid if there is a breach of contract. The amount is specifically stated in the contract. The amount must be reasonable, or else the courts will likely throw out the award.

- *Payment terms.* This clause states the prices that will be paid, and any adjustment factors, such as pricing changes based on the passage of time or changes in the amount of units purchased. Prices may also be adjusted based on changes in pricing indexes or foreign exchange rates.

- *Performance.* Depending on the nature of the contract, there may be a clause outlining the circumstances under which a supplier is considered to have unusually poor or excellent performance, and the penalties or extra compensation associated with each condition. For example, an engineering firm constructing a runway could be penalized for late delivery and paid a bonus for early delivery.

- *Purchase orders.* This clause establishes the linkage between the contract and any purchase orders issued by the buyer to a supplier during the term of an agreement. The usual terms indicate that any purchase orders issued during the term of the contract are assumed to fall under the terms and conditions set forth in the contract. There may also be language regarding what to do if the terms in a purchase order vary from the contract terms (the contract terms typically override the purchase order terms).

- *Risk of loss.* If a supplier is being asked to stock inventory at a buyer location, a clause should define which of the parties is responsible for any inventory damage or losses occurring while the inventory is being stored at the buyer location.

- *Severability.* This is a boilerplate statement that the rest of the contract is still enforceable even if one or more clauses are subsequently proven to be void or unenforceable.

- *Stop work order.* This clause may be triggered by the owner to stop work by the seller when conditions arise that could damage the work product, endanger facilities, or present safety issues for workers. When this clause is triggered, the seller is responsible for resolving the indicated issues. Conditions that might trigger a stop work order include a lack of quality control procedures, work being conducted in violation of contract specifications, the use of non-conforming materials, and the use of drawings that have not yet been approved by the buyer.

- *Subcontracting.* The buyer may not want a subcontractor to handle the work it is assigning to a supplier. This can be a particular issue if the goods being produced have unusually tight tolerances, and the buyer is uncertain of the ability of a subcontractor to deliver goods within the designated specifications.

- *Termination.* This clause states the conditions under which either party can terminate the contract. This clause is always worth a close examination, to determine how tightly the parties are being bound to the terms of the contract. There may be additional language stating any payments to be made in the event of an early contract termination; for example, the buyer may need to pay the supplier if a certain purchasing volume was not attained as of the termination date.

- *Time is of the essence.* This clause is included when the contracted work must be completed by a specific date. The clause is intended to enforce strict compliance with the project due date, after which incentive payments are voided and liquidated damages may apply.

- *Transfer of ownership.* If a supplier is being asked to stock inventory at a buyer location, a clause should define the circumstances under which there is a transfer of ownership from the supplier to the buyer.

Footer

- *Signatures.* Authorized signatories for both parties sign and date the agreement. The key point here is "authorized," since an unauthorized person could sign a contract. Accordingly, it is customary for both parties to state their job titles in the signature block.

Any of the preceding terms and conditions may refer to a schedule that is attached to the back of a contract. These schedules provide additional detail that clarifies the basic terms, such as the specific measurement calculations to be used to evaluate the performance of a supplier, or the unit volumes at which volume discounts will begin to apply. The schedules deserve at least as much attention as the main clauses of the contract, since they are the least likely to be boilerplate; instead, they will have been written specifically for a contract. The types of schedules integrated into a contract can vary substantially; the following are more likely to be found in a purchase contract:

- Expected unit volumes to be ordered
- Prices to be paid and mechanisms for adjusting those prices
- Product quality assurance guidelines
- Product specifications or statement of work
- Required lead times for orders
- Shipping methods to be used

The negotiation of each paragraph in the terms and conditions of a contract can require an inordinate amount of time. To make better use of the purchasing staff's time, it is better to adopt the industry-standard terms and conditions, and then only adjust those specific items that need to be tailored to a specific purchase.

Commercial Terms

The contract terms and conditions described in the preceding section can be considered the basic, low-level legal minutiae of a contract. They are simply a requirement of doing business, and are always present in order to deal with a range of issues that commonly arise. The more important part of a contract is its commercial terms. These terms address the quality, price, delivery, and other key aspects of an arrangement that are unique to that arrangement.

Commercial terms are not boilerplate. Instead, they are based on a lengthy discussion of the business arrangement that both parties are contemplating entering. In particular, commercial terms should be crafted only after there has been a discussion of the full range of conditions that may arise during the contract term, and the burdens that these conditions may place on either party. The ideal commercial terms are ones that will keep a contract from failing, where the terms will change to accommodate a party that is being negatively impacted by an alteration in conditions. For example:

- Rather than requiring the buyer to purchase a minimum of 1,000,000 units in each of the next ten years, the requirement starts at 1,000,000 units and then declines by 10% per year. Doing so accommodates the buyer, which may be increasingly uncertain about its need for 1,000,000 units in the later years of the contract.
- A utility needs a long-term source of coal, but the supplier is concerned about being locked into a long-term fixed price arrangement. To accommodate the supplier, the contract states that the contract price will be compared to the

market price at annual intervals, with a maximum price adjustment of 5% occurring at each of these intervals. Doing so mitigates the total amount of the maximum price change for the utility, while providing some relief to the supplier.

If it seems like a waste of time to go over all possible contingencies with a supplier as part of the contract development, consider that *not* doing so may lead to a lawsuit, which will be far more expensive.

The Employee or Contractor Designation

An area of particular concern when developing a contract is to clearly identify whether a supplier is considered a buyer employee. If an individual is considered an employee, then any intellectual property developed by that person becomes the property of the buyer. If an individual is instead considered an independent contractor, then ownership of this property is less clear, and should be defined further in the contract.

To determine whether a person can be classified as an independent contractor, review the entire working relationship between the buyer and the person, and arrive at a decision based on the complete body of evidence. There are three categories of facts to consider, which are:

- *Behavioral control.* A person is an employee if the business has the right to direct and control how the person does the task for which he was hired. The amount of control is based on the level of instruction regarding such issues as when and where to work, what equipment to use, which employees to use, where to buy supplies, what sequence of tasks to follow, and so forth. Behavioral control can include training by the buyer to perform services in a particular way.
- *Financial control.* Facts indicative of financial control by the buyer are the extent to which a worker is reimbursed for business expenses, the amount of investment by the worker in the business, the extent to which the worker sells his services to other parties, whether the amount paid to the person is based on time worked rather than for a work product, and whether the worker can participate in a profit or loss.
- *Type of relationship.* A person is more likely to be considered an independent contractor if there is a written contract describing the relationship of the parties, the business does not provide benefits to the person, the relationship is not permanent, and the services performed are not a key aspect of the regular business of the buyer.

EXAMPLE

Mr. David Stringer is a securities attorney who specializes in the issuance of bonds. He has been paid on an hourly basis for the last ten years by his sole client, Heavy Lift Corporation (HLC), and is reimbursed by HLC for expenses incurred. The CFO of HLC does not attempt to control the work habits of Mr. Stringer. There is no contract between the two parties; instead,

Mr. Stringer simply issues an invoice to HLC at the end of each month, and the company pays it. HLC does not pay any benefits to Mr. Stringer. HLC is not in the business of selling bonds – it only does so periodically in order to raise capital.

The cumulative evidence in this situation is in favor of Mr. Stringer being an independent contractor. HLC does not exercise behavioral control, though there is some evidence of financial control that would be reduced if Mr. Stringer had any additional clients. The type of relationship is more firmly in favor of independent contractor status, since HLC does not pay benefits and Mr. Stringer's area of specialization is outside of the regular business of the company.

EXAMPLE

Waylon Price has signed a contract with Milford Sound to provide concrete pouring services for several of Milford's public stadium projects. Under the terms of the contract, Mr. Price's firm will be paid a flat fee once specific tasks have been completed, and is liable for any subsequent issues with the concrete through a one-year warranty period. Mr. Price carries workers' compensation insurance for his business, and he employs several people. Mr. Price is an independent contractor.

EXAMPLE

Hubble Corporation lays off Red Miller, and then agrees to pay him a flat fee to design trajectory tracking software for one of Hubble's telescopes. Hubble does not provide Mr. Miller with any specific work instructions, and only sets a target date for delivery of the software. He is not required to attend any meetings of the programming department. He has signed an agreement with Hubble, which specifically states that he is an independent contractor, and will receive no benefits from the company. Mr. Miller is an independent contractor.

Contract Pricing Arrangements

The type of pricing incorporated into a contract can vary substantially, depending on the extent of risk sharing between the parties. In the following sub-sections, we note the different pricing arrangements that can be incorporated into a contract, with commentary on the effects of each one and the situations in which they are used.

Firm Fixed Price

The most common pricing arrangement is the firm fixed price, where (as the name implies) the supplier commits to provide goods or services in exchange for the payment of a specific, unvarying price. Buyers like to use firm fixed pricing, because all risks of cost fluctuations are shifted to the supplier. These fluctuations can include the costs of new labor contracts with unions, spikes in commodity prices, and adverse foreign exchange rates, so a supplier may be taking on a substantial risk of loss under this arrangement. However, suppliers can also benefit handsomely from a firm fixed price, if all of the risk variables turn in favor of the supplier. Also, if there are few or

31

no competitors to drive down the price, a supplier can bid a firm fixed price that guarantees it a generous profit.

Besides the offloading of risk, buyers also like the firm fixed price arrangement because there is no need to review the costs of the supplier (as is the case with the following cost plus pricing arrangement). Instead, the buyer simply confirms that the contracted goods or services have been received, and then pays the designated price.

The firm fixed price concept can be risky for either party when incorporated into a long-term contract, depending on future changes in market conditions. For example, a utility may contract for a 20-year supply of coal from a coal mine, at a price that is 10% below the current market price. Initially, this arrangement benefits the buyer. However, a few years later, the federal government places a tax on coal, which reduces demand and thereby cuts its market price to a level 20% below the contract price. At this point, the contract favors the supplier over the buyer. Thus, the use of this type of pricing over long periods of time can have unintended effects for the participants.

When a firm fixed price arrangement clearly places the risk on the supplier, it is not uncommon for the supplier to then boost its bid price. The intent of doing so is to give it some profit cushion to offset the potential risk of loss that it would otherwise incur.

Firm fixed price arrangements work best for short-term delivery schedules, where it is unlikely that market prices will change significantly.

Fixed Price with Adjustments

As just noted, the basic problem with a firm fixed price arrangement is that the supplier is taking on a number of risks that could result in losses. There are several ways to equalize the sharing of these risks by modifying the contract. Consider the following alternatives:

- *Escalation clause*. The contractual price to be paid is compared to a price index at regular intervals. If the linked price index changes, then so too does the contractual price. The assumption is that the price index will increase, which allows a supplier to charge higher prices. However, it is not impossible that the price index could decline, resulting in lower contractual rates. An escalation clause is fair to both parties when a long-term pricing arrangement is contemplated.

- *Incentives clause*. A variety of incentive payments for a supplier can be built into a fixed price contract. The intent is to give the supplier a good reason to increase its production efficiencies or to accelerate the delivery of goods. If certain targets are met, this triggers additional payments to the supplier. This clause can work well when the buyer expects a supplier to reduce its costs over time as it improves a production process, and wants to share in these cost reductions.

- *Revision clause*. There are situations where the production process for a new product is so new that the supplier cannot create a reasonable bid price for the work. Perhaps there is a new process that has only been attempted in a small pilot plant, and no one knows what costs will be incurred to produce at a higher level. Whatever the case may be, the parties can insert a clause in the contract to re-examine the supplier's production costs once a certain production volume has been achieved, and re-set the fixed price at that time. The resulting pricing revision may be complex, so it makes sense to include a schedule that provides additional detail about the revision calculation, as well as an example revision scenario.

Cost plus Pricing

Cost plus pricing is a price-setting method under which the direct material cost is added to the direct labor cost and overhead cost for a product, after which a markup percentage is added in order to derive the contract price. In a contract, the buyer reimburses the supplier for all costs incurred and also pays a negotiated profit in addition to the costs incurred.

EXAMPLE

A government agency contracts with Failsafe Containment to develop a containment vessel for a new fusion reactor model. The work involves a large amount of research and is highly risky, so Failsafe insists on a cost plus pricing arrangement, where it is guaranteed a 6% profit on all costs incurred.

Over the course of the contract, Failsafe incurs costs of $50,000,000, which includes related overhead costs of $8,000,000. The government reimburses Failsafe for the full $50,000,000, plus a 6% profit, which is another $3,000,000.

The following are disadvantages of using the cost plus pricing method, from the perspective of the buyer:

- *Assured contract profits*. Any supplier is willing to accept this method for a contractual agreement with a customer, since it is assured of having its costs reimbursed and of making a profit. There is no risk of loss on such a contract for the supplier. Instead, the buyer takes on all risk.
- *Contract cost overruns*. The supplier has no incentive to curtail its expenditures - on the contrary, it will likely include as many costs as possible in the contract so that it can be reimbursed. This is a particular problem when a supplier has a large amount of corporate and factory overhead, where it is difficult to determine how these costs can be allocated. Thus, a contractual arrangement should include cost-reduction incentives for the supplier.

From a paperwork perspective, cost plus pricing has the following advantages for both parties:

- *Justifiable*. In cases where the supplier must persuade its customer of the need for a price increase, the supplier can point to an increase in its costs as the reason for the price increase.

- *Simple.* It is quite easy to derive a billable price using this method, though both parties should define the overhead allocation method in order to be consistent in calculating how much overhead will be charged to a contract.

When entering into a cost plus arrangement, the classification of which costs are allowable should be carefully reviewed. It is possible that the terms of the contract are so restrictive that the supplier must exclude many costs from reimbursement, and so can potentially incur a loss.

A cost plus arrangement works well when the buyer and supplier have a long history of working together, since this means they are more likely to have mutually agreed to a policy regarding which costs are to be billed, and the buyer trusts the supplier in regard to which costs are submitted.

A variation on the cost plus pricing arrangement is the cost plus fixed-fee contract. Under this approach, the supplier is reimbursed for all qualifying costs incurred, and is also paid a fixed profit amount that is based on the original budgeted cost of the item to be constructed. This variation is usually not recommended from the perspective of the buyer, since there is no incentive for a supplier to reduce its costs – instead, all risks have been shifted to the buyer.

Time and Materials Pricing

Time and materials pricing is used in service industries to bill customers for a standard labor rate per hour used, plus the actual cost of materials used. The standard labor rate per hour being billed does not necessarily relate to the underlying cost of the labor; instead, it may be based on the market rate for the services of someone having a certain skill set. Thus, a computer technician may bill out at $100 per hour, while costing $30 per hour, while a cable television mechanic may only bill out at $80 per hour, despite costing the same amount per hour. The cost of materials charged to the customer is for any materials actually used during the performance of services for the customer. This cost may be at the supplier's actual cost, or it may be a marked-up cost that includes a fee for the overhead cost associated with ordering, handling, and holding the materials in stock.

Under the time and materials pricing methodology, a single hourly rate may be charged irrespective of the experience level of the person performing the services, but usually there are different rates for different experience levels within the company. Thus, an associate consultant will have a lower billing rate than a consulting manager, who in turn has a lower billing rate than a consulting partner.

Industries in which time and materials pricing are used include:

- Accounting, auditing, and tax services
- Consulting services
- Legal work
- Medical services
- Vehicle repair

If a company chooses to base its labor rate under time and materials pricing on its underlying costs, rather than the market rate, it can do so by adding together the following:

- The cost of compensation, payroll taxes, and benefits per hour for the employee providing billable services
- An allocation of general overhead costs
- An additional factor to account for the proportion of expected unbillable time

---

EXAMPLE

Hammer Industries has an equipment repair group that charges out its staff at a level that covers the cost of labor, plus a profit factor. In the past year, Hammer incurred $2,000,000 of salary expenses, plus $140,000 of payroll taxes, $300,000 of employee benefits, and $500,000 of office expenses; this totaled $2,940,000 of expenses for the year. In the past year, the company had 30,000 billable hours, which is roughly what it expects to bill out in the near future. Hammer wants the division to earn a 20% profit. Based on this information, the division charges $122.50 per hour for each of its repair personnel. The calculation of the labor price per hour is:

$2,940,000 annual costs ÷ (1 - 20% profit percentage) = $3,675,000 revenue needed

$3,675,000 revenue needed ÷ 30,000 billable hours = $122.50 billing rate

---

The following are disadvantages to using the time and materials pricing method, from the perspective of the buyer:

- *High prices.* The billing rates charged may far exceed the underlying costs of the supplier, resulting in inordinately high fees.
- *High risk situations.* This pricing method is similar to cost plus pricing, in that a supplier has no responsibility for the outcome of the work product, thereby shifting the risk of the final outcome of the contract to the buyer.

If a buyer is willing to negotiate, it is possible to substantially reduce the hourly billing rates being charged, especially if the buyer is planning to pay for many hours of work. If so, include a pricing schedule in the contract that notes the percentage discounts that will be applied as the unit volume of hours worked increases. The following are additional possibilities for controlling the price paid:

- Include a "not to exceed" cap in the contract, so that the buyer will not be egregiously overbilled.
- Negotiate the maximum margin added to any materials supplied under the contract.
- Insist on periodic reviews of project status and the activities of all billable personnel, to monitor project progress. This can be coupled with a termination

clause that allows the buyer to escape from a contract if project progress is inadequate.

The Escalation Clause

When a contract is likely to run for several years, the seller will likely be subject to the risk of price increases. These increases may be specific to the work being performed, such as increases in the cost of labor, materials, and equipment rentals, as well as higher interest rates on borrowed funds. To protect the seller, it may be necessary to insert an escalation clause into the contract, allowing for a reasonable adjustment in prices over time that is fair to both parties. Rather than attempting to estimate future costs, the clause instead increases prices based on indexes that measure changes in future prices in comparison to a base period.

The use of an index to adjust prices still places the seller at some risk, since indexes are based on general prices across several industries, and so may not properly account for pricing spikes for the labor and materials for which the seller must pay in order to complete a contract. Thus, the seller bears the risk of any differences between local inflation rates and the general inflation rates incorporated in the relevant index.

An escalation clause could also incorporate text that allows the seller to adjust prices when there are changes in the applicable laws and regulations. For example, a contractor working on a high-rise apartment complex in a city will be severely impacted when local regulations mandate that no work can be performed on weekends – thereby forcing the contractor to pay overtime during the remaining days in order to complete the work on time.

Summary of Pricing Arrangements

The variety of pricing arrangements available represents a full continuum of risk management possibilities. Firm fixed pricing shifts risk to the supplier, while any cost reimbursement arrangement shifts risk onto the buyer. A buyer might be tempted to always use firm fixed pricing, especially when it is large enough to impose pricing conditions on a small supplier. This is not always a good idea, since it imposes a burden on the supplier base. The realization of any of these risks could result in a financially weaker group of suppliers, which hurts a buyer in the long run. A wiser approach is to examine the inherent risks in each contract, and engage in mutual risk mitigation and hedging activities with suppliers – especially those suppliers considered critical to the welfare of the buyer. This approach can also engender a notable amount of supplier loyalty.

It is entirely possible that one or even both parties to a pricing arrangement in a contract will be confused by it. A simple description of a pricing arrangement may be subject to interpretation, which could result in serious disputes between the parties. To avoid this problem, consider adding a schedule to the contract that clarifies the arrangement in greater detail. For example, it could describe the date and source of any inflation index to be used to alter prices, the definitions of each element of a pricing formula, and an example that includes one or more hypothetical pricing situations.

Contract Payment Arrangements

Sellers are usually paid when the associated goods or services are delivered. However, this is less likely to be the case when an extended period will be required for performance. When a long performance period is expected, the seller will want to be paid prior to the completion date. This is especially necessary when the seller has to incur substantial initial start-up costs, such as for the materials on a construction project.

When a portion of the price is paid up-front or near the front end of a project, one must review the seller's initial projected expenditures to ensure that the amount being paid is not in excess of the costs incurred. Otherwise, the seller is not taking on any risk of loss, and so has less incentive to complete all performance on a timely basis. A better approach from the perspective of the buyer is to establish a retainage in the contract, which is paid only after the buyer is satisfied with the seller's performance. The retainage amount should be sufficiently large to incentivize the seller to fully perform under the terms of the contract.

In cases where the seller does not have a substantial amount of cash to fund its operations, it may be necessary for the buyer to arrange payments so that the seller has sufficient cash on hand to fund its operations. This may require the buyer to pay out more cash during the front end of a contract than would normally be the case.

Contract Templates

A buyer could use a standard contract template for all of its purchasing requirements. However, the terms and conditions associated with one arrangement, such as the purchase of commodities, might not apply to an arrangement involving the design of a new process flow, or a strategic consulting agreement. Consequently, it can make sense to develop a set of contracts that are applicable to different purchasing situations, each with a different set of terms and conditions. This is done in order to standardize contracts for specific purposes, which minimizes the amount of contract customization that may be required. For example, there may be separate contract formats for the purchase of goods, services, and transportation. Each of these standard contracts should contain clauses that answer the following questions:

- Does it identify what is being acquired?
- Does it address the shipment and installation of the item being acquired?
- Does the recipient need to examine and formally accept the delivered goods or services?
- If the delivered goods or services do not meet expectations, what are the consequences for the seller?
- If there is a need for a product or service warranty, what should it cover, and for what period of time?

Duration-Based Contractual Issues

The many terms, conditions, and other clauses noted in an earlier section are mostly applicable to longer-term contractual arrangements. In these arrangements, the intent is for a buyer to develop relations with suppliers that are expected to last through a number of purchases, possibly including the sharing of intellectual property. These can be rewarding arrangements, but require much more time to craft a contract that accommodates the needs of both parties. Conversely, a short-term contract is usually needed to fulfill a one-time requirement, after which there is no expectation that a buyer will continue to need the services of a supplier. Given the impact of these different scenarios, we include in the following table the contractual issues to consider, based on contract duration.

Contractual Issues Based on Contract Duration

	Short-Term Contract	Long-Term Contract
Commitment	There is no expectation that a buyer will need to deal with a supplier again	There is an expectation that the two parties will work together on a regular basis
Industry capacity	When the industry is nearing full capacity, suppliers are more interested in short-term contracts, so that they can charge at the higher spot rates	When an industry has lots of excess capacity, suppliers are more willing to lock in long-term deals, thereby assuring the use of some portion of their available capacity
Operating cost information	The buyer does not expect a supplier to share any operating cost information with it, with the intent of setting prices based on underlying costs	The supplier is willing to share its operating cost information with the buyer, so that the parties can jointly determine a reasonable price to pay, as well as opportunities for cost reduction
Product development	Raw materials and components are purchased in standard configurations	The two parties work together to create new components and non-standard parts, possibly jointly developing intellectual property
Production schedule	The buyer does not intend to share its production schedule with the supplier	The buyer insists that the supplier continually accesses its production schedule, in order to determine when and where goods are to be delivered
Purchasing centralization	The buyer may only purchase a single item from a supplier	The buyer is interested in placing orders for multiple types of goods with a supplier
Reserved capacity	The supplier will ship to the buyer when it can find the time to fill an order	The supplier is willing to set aside capacity for the buyer, which gives the buyer preferential shipment dates; this can be critical when raw material supplies can be easily disrupted

	Short-Term Contract	Long-Term Contract
Supplier finances	The buyer is not overly interested in the long-term viability of the supplier, only in obtaining low prices for commodity items	The buyer anticipates such a close relationship that the supplier must have a robust financial situation; the buyer cannot afford to have the supplier go bankrupt
Supplier progressiveness	If the supplier does not appear interested in continuing improvement, it cannot reduce its costs or develop more advanced products	When the supplier's management team is constantly driving toward more efficient operations and enhanced products, the buyer will benefit from its pricing and product enhancements
Technology sharing	Neither party expects to have access to the technology of the other party	Both parties expect to use each other's intellectual property to develop cutting-edge goods; this is especially useful when doing so can block a supplier's technology from competitors
Unpredictable volumes	When the buyer is not certain of the volume of units needed, it is more likely to use short-term contracts until the volume requirements are clearer	When there is a high level of predictability in the number of units needed, it is safer to obtain them through a long-term contract where the buyer is obligated to buy in certain volumes

The points raised in the table should make it clear that only a minority of contracts need to be set up as long-term arrangements. The purchasing team should discuss the pros and cons of a long-term arrangement before engaging in any discussions with a supplier to do so. In many cases, the advantages of a long-term contract will not be apparent, in which case it will be more cost-effective to write a short-term contract using mostly boilerplate terms and conditions.

A particular concern when selecting a supplier for a long-term contract is the risk of a "false positive," which arises when the wrong supplier is picked for a long-term contract. If so, the purchasing team may find that a supplier is unable to deliver on time, produces sub-standard goods, is not willing to work together on product development, and so forth. This is a major concern when a contract mandates that the two parties work together for a number of years. This concern may introduce a great deal of hesitation about entering into long-term contractual arrangements. A reasonable way to allay this concern is to first work with suppliers on short-term joint collaboration arrangements, and only progress to a long-term contract when the management team is convinced that doing so presents few downside risks.

Summary

Contracts are an essential part of the documentation generated by the purchasing department, and are the basis for many of its transactions. Given their importance, the purchasing professional should be familiar with the basic contents of a contract, when a contract should be used, and what types of pricing arrangements it should encompass.

Chapter 3
Contracting Risks

Introduction

When entering into a contract arrangement, the contract manager should consider all significant contracting risks. A *contracting risk* is an uncertainty that, if it were to occur, would adversely impact the contracting objectives. The contract manager should identify those contracting risks that are material, and design the request for proposals (as discussed in the following chapter) to mitigate them.

Types of Contracting Risks

Some contracting risks can arise from the contracting process itself, while other risks are more closely associated with the type of project under consideration or the technology to be used within it. Generally, the types of contracting risks to be aware of are as follows:

- *That the estimated cost of a purchase is exceeded.* This is most common when custom-designed goods are being obtained, or when the technology incorporated into the product is extremely leading-edge. The military routinely experiences this problem, since it is constantly incorporating the latest technology into its weapons systems, resulting in massive cost overruns.
- *That contracted work is not completed on time.* This is most likely to occur when there are multiple constraints on a project, any of which can severely delay the work. For example, an acoustical product has a large rare earth component, which can only be sourced from a few mines outside of the country. In the event of a pandemic or other event that closes national borders, the buyer will not be able to import the raw materials that it needs.
- *That contracted goods or services do not meet quality thresholds.* This is especially common when management is trying to keep costs low by contracting to the lowest-cost suppliers. These suppliers can only turn a profit if the provided goods are of the lowest possible quality levels. This is also a concern when shifting to a new supplier whose quality levels have not been sufficiently investigated.
- *That required materials cannot be obtained.* This is a particular problem when key components are in short supply. For example, there are periodic shortages of computer chips that can halt the production of many goods, ranging from automobiles to clothes washers.
- *That the goods are damaged in transit.* This can be caused by improper packaging by the seller, as well as by rough road conditions. It is a particular concern when sourcing from third-world countries where the road networks are poorly-developed, placing goods in transit at more risk.

- *That employees or third parties are injured during the work.* This is a significant issue during construction projects, especially when the construction is being performed by smaller contractors that pay less attention to worker safety.
- *That uncontrollable events occur, such as negative weather conditions.* This is an increasingly important issue as climate change impacts weather conditions in all areas, triggering or enhancing floods, fires, and hurricanes that damage facilities and stop the transport of goods. Other non-weather events, such as earthquakes, can have a similar negative impact.
- *That first-of-a-kind activities are being conducted.* This risk arises when bleeding-edge technologies are involved, or simply when a buyer is trying to integrate a new system into its processes within which it has no prior experience.

Contracting Risk Mitigation Activities

There are several ways to mitigate the contracting risks just noted. We describe some of the better options in the following bullet points:

- *Buy based on experience.* It can make sense to favor the most experienced suppliers when awarding contracts. These parties have experienced a broad range of issues within their chosen fields, and so are in the best position to watch out for and correct problems. That being said, it can sometimes make sense to try out new suppliers if they offer new solutions that more established suppliers do not.
- *Continually monitor progress.* Contract managers need to monitor seller progress on a regular basis to catch performance problems as soon as possible. Doing so allows for more time in which to come up with workarounds to keep the seller's delivery on time.
- *Delay the introduction of new technology.* When technology has not yet been used in the application or product being contemplated, it can make sense to wait and let some other party work with the concept and iron out any bugs that may arise.
- *Develop a comprehensive scope of work.* An essential risk mitigation technique is to allocate a significant amount of time to the development of the scope of work. When this has been clearly defined, there should be little remaining wiggle room over which the buyer and seller might argue.
- *Evaluate requirements based on availability.* Conduct an assessment early in the planning process to determine whether the materials and expertise needed to conduct the work are readily available. If not, it may make sense to alter the design of the work to use more readily accessible resources.
- *Initially use several contractors.* An expensive approach is to hire two sellers to initially engage in the same work, and then pick the best of the two once the buyer has evaluated their initial progress in scoping out the work. Any best practices developed by the losing seller can then be adopted by the

winning party. This is only cost-effective for very large and expensive projects, where it is essential to devise the best up-front planning process for how the work is to be completed.

- *Monitor key activities.* Install measurement systems to monitor those activities identified as being bottlenecks, or which are considered the most likely to fail. The measurement effort should be targeted, so that no time is wasted monitoring routine activities.

- *Obtain a seller warranty.* The buyer can insist on a substantial warranty from the seller that covers those problems most likely to arise, and extending over a reasonable proportion of the expected usage period of the item being acquired.

- *Resolve non-conformance issues.* When issues are found that breach the terms of a contract, have a process in place to investigate and resolve them at once. This is a critical task, since the resolutions may require a recasting of the project timeline – which may then impact the timing of other activities.

- *Set realistic budgets.* Provide sufficient funding for a project. Doing so ensures that enough people and other resources will be assigned to it, and that the buyer does not throw out the best suppliers because their prices are too high.

- *Set realistic schedules.* There are more risks associated with compressed project timelines, so be generous in setting the dates by which performance is supposed to be complete. When this is not possible, then assign more staff to closely monitor progress toward completion and identify potential bottlenecks, so at least there will be an early warning system if a completion date is unlikely to be met.

- *Source locally.* When there are risks associated with the transport of goods, source locally to mitigate those risks. In essence, parts coming from across town are more likely to arrive at the buyer's facility than parts being produced on the other side of the world. However, one must balance the mitigation of transport risks against a possible loss of quality if local suppliers are substandard.

- *Use experienced managers.* Always assign the most experienced contract managers to the most complex contracting situations. These people have enough experience to anticipate and guard against most problems that may be encountered. More junior contract managers should be assigned to less-complex contracting situations, or be assigned to complex contracting situations in a supporting role.

- *Work from a standard RFP template.* By using a standard template, one can be assured that all standard provisions are included in the document. Conversely, developing an RFP from scratch every time is not recommended, since it is too easy to inadvertently leave out critical clauses.

Megaproject Issues

A megaproject is generally considered to be any project that costs at least $1 billion. Common megaprojects are subways, power plants, airport terminals, pipelines, and sports complexes. These projects routinely go over budget, sometimes by many multiples of the original cost estimates, and may be completed years later than their targeted completion dates. There are real issues that cause these massive overages, such as the impact of new regulations, court cases brought by negatively impacted parties, and disputes over who is authorized to oversee and make changes to the work. Perhaps the most central issue is that project complexity increases with the size of the project, making megaprojects exceedingly difficult to manage properly. To gain better control over these difficult projects, we suggest following these best practices:

- *Study comparable projects.* Conduct a detailed review of similar projects that have been completed within the past decade, looking in particular for problems encountered and how they were dealt with. This may include site visits, in order to discuss issues in detail with the people who worked on these projects.
- *Share risk with suppliers.* Selectively issue more cost-plus contracts to suppliers, rather than fixed-price contracts. Doing so moves some of the risk back to the buyer and away from suppliers, who will therefore be more willing to discuss changes to the project as it proceeds.
- *Identify areas of uncertainty.* A typical megaproject will contain many areas with little risk, since they incorporate techniques that have been used many times in the past. In addition, there will be a much smaller number of high-risk areas. These latter areas need to be identified early in the project and monitored much more closely than the low-risk areas. It will be more useful to use cost-plus arrangements with any suppliers involved in high-risk areas, since these are the areas most likely to require a higher degree of collaboration and risk sharing with suppliers.
- *Avoid bleeding-edge solutions.* Only install technologies and construction techniques that have been proven to work in related projects, and preferably over a lengthy period of time. Conversely, avoid any cutting-edge solutions that may sound good, but which have not yet been proven to work at scale. Otherwise, a new approach that is central to the project design may fail, resulting in massive delays and cost overruns. When there is uncertainty that cannot be avoided, consider running a pilot project elsewhere and in advance of the main project, to identify issues and figure out how to resolve them.
- *Develop a change culture.* Encourage the many project teams involved in the project to be flexible in how they deal with any problems encountered, rather than following the original plan in an excessively rigid manner. This will likely require a deliberate approach to staffing project teams with only the highest-quality people; the added cost of these personnel will be more than offset by the resulting project savings.

- *Create an innovation team.* Have a dedicated group within the project team solely focused on finding and implementing innovation enhancements in every aspect of the project, for its entire duration. This group should also poll suppliers, to see if they can contribute any ideas to the effort. This concept can be enhanced by developing a formal system to accumulate and report on the progress of any ideas generated.
- *Consult with subsequent operators.* Those charged with ongoing management of the completed project may have a strong interest in reducing operating costs, so consult with them early in the project to see if any operational enhancements can be built into the project that will reduce long-term costs.

Summary

Proper consideration of contracting risks is essential, especially when the cost of a contract is substantial, or when a favorable outcome is key to a buyer's strategy. In these situations, the contract manager should review the circumstances of a proposed purchase to identify the most critical risks, and develop a plan for how to mitigate them to the greatest extent possible.

Chapter 4
The Request for Proposals

Introduction

A *request for proposals* (RFP) is a business document that announces a project, describes it, and solicits bids from qualified sellers to complete it. It contains all technical, legal, administrative, and scheduling requirements for a bidding party to prepare a cost estimate and a schedule for when the mandated work can be performed. Many large projects begin with an RFP. The delivery of an RFP constitutes the first interaction that a buyer has with a seller, so it is essential that the document is properly prepared. If not, the buyer will have to spend extra time issuing clarifications to sellers, which may have a downstream impact on the success of the eventual purchase. In this chapter, we cover the planning for and content of an RFP, as well as several related issues.

The Need for Teams

Before we begin with the discussion of the request for proposals, this is a good place in which to note how the contracting process should be structured. This is not a good time to insert a silo structure, where one person completes a task and then throws it over the wall to the person who has responsibility for the next step. When this happens, there is a loss of knowledge in regard to what went before, resulting in inefficiencies and errors in each successive step of the contracting process.

There are several ways to get around this inherent inefficiency. One is to assign responsibility for all aspects of an RFP and the following contract to a single manager, so that any failures in the process can be ascribed to that person. In addition, the formulation and management of a contract should be assigned to a team, which works together on all aspects of the work. By making the process a team effort, it is more likely that the most essential issues are identified and addressed early in the contracting process. This means that significant losses are less likely to be incurred as the associated work is conducted.

Planning for an RFP

The planning process for an RFP begins when a substantial expenditure is identified for products or services. These purchases can cover a broad range, such as the construction of a building, the purchase of raw materials for a production process, or the development of software for a major company process.

The people who initially determine the requirements for an RFP are those managers directly responsible for the area most directly impacted by the planned purchase. This group needs to develop a scope for the project, from which it can devise a budget and timeline for completion. If this analysis reveals that the organization does not have the in-house resources or production capabilities to complete the work, then the purchasing and legal departments are brought in to develop a detailed purchasing plan – of which the first output is the RFP. The development of a well-crafted RFP requires a large amount of cross-departmental work, so the sooner this team can be brought together, the sooner the RFP can be issued.

The first step in the process is to prepare a project plan that schedules all milestones related to the RFP, including document development and review, document release, bidders' meetings, proposal evaluation, contract negotiation, and the issuance of purchase orders. The plan dates may need to be compressed in order to support the requirements of the underlying project. This plan is also useful for scheduling in-house staffing to the RFP process, to ensure that there are sufficient qualified personnel available to complete each phase of the work.

> **Tip:** The project plan needs to be continually updated with the latest information, so that the contract manager can spot any changes that will require additional procurements or changes to existing procurement plans. This means that a dedicated staff will likely be needed to provide ongoing updates to the plan, as well as timely notifications to the contract manager.

A particular concern is to identify any long lead-time items, or materials for which the supplier capacity is limited, so that the purchasing process can be accelerated for these items. The contract manager will need to be particularly cognizant of the procurement process for these items, so that they do not delay the underlying project. In cases where the scheduling is extremely tight on long lead-time items, it can make sense to avoid the RFP process entirely and simply sole source them in order to be ensured of prompt delivery.

A follow-on to the lead time issue is whether any incentives will be built into the RFP, such as awards for delivering the completed product or service prior to a specific date. Incentives should only be offered when the resulting benefit to the buyer equals or exceeds the amount of the incentive payment. Further, penalties can be imposed when the seller cannot meet its obligations by a specific date.

Procurement Strategy

It is quite likely that the number of potential sellers of the goods or services needed by the buyer is quite limited. For example, when the buyer is a city government that wants to build a new parking garage for city hall, there may be few contractors with adequate experience in such construction, and especially within the city's geographic area. Or, the number of contractors that can build a satellite for a weather photo processing company will be quite low, given the level of expertise needed to construct such a device. Generally, the number of potential sellers will decline as the projected cost of a procurement increases, simply because there are so few sellers with the skills and experience to successfully deliver on large contracts. Given this constraint, it is likely that the procurement strategy adopted by a contract manager will be tailored to the number of available contractors, as well as the cost of the contract. This means that a contract manager can select from the following four procurement strategies, depending on the circumstances:

1. *High contract cost, few available sellers*. These sellers are usually large, with highly targeted areas of expertise. It can be difficult to initiate a price war between these types of sellers, since they are in a good position to select from the best offers being made to them by buyers. In this situation, the best procurement strategy may be to focus on which seller has sufficient capacity to supply the buyer within its required time frame.
2. *High contract cost, many available sellers*. When there are more prospective sellers, a good strategy is to set up a pricing competition among a group of sellers. This is a good area in which to issue an RFP, so that the bidding process can be properly structured.
3. *Low contract cost, few available sellers*. When the contract cost is lower but there are only a few suppliers, it will be difficult to obtain a reduced price. A better strategy is to offer a seller a longer-term deal, perhaps involving a series of purchases, in exchange for a somewhat reduced price. The higher level of order assurance may be a tempting offer to a seller that wants to fill its order backlog well into the future.
4. *Low contract cost, many available sellers*. When the purchasing cost is low and there are many sellers, it can make sense to initially conduct a competitive bidding process, and then sole source subsequent purchases to the winning seller. Prices can be kept low through volume purchasing arrangements, while the administrative cost of issuing subsequent RFPs is avoided. Occasional meetings between the parties can be used to evaluate the relationship and adjust pricing as necessary.

Within these four general procurement strategies, the contract manager might elect to pursue several alternative methods to solicit proposals from prospective sellers. One approach is *competitive bidding*, where a number of sellers bid against each other, presumably resulting in the lowest possible price. For competitive bidding to operate properly, there must be a sufficient number of sellers interested in submitting bids, a mechanism for providing them all with sufficient information about the goods or services required (the RFP), and enough time to complete a thorough bidding process. Of these criteria, having sufficient time to conduct a thorough bidding process may be the greatest constraint, since multiple months may be required to complete it. Given the timing constraint, competitive bidding is really only possible for larger purchases for which there is no immediate need for rapid completion.

There are several potential problems with competitive bidding. First, if there are few prospective sellers interested in submitting bids, then the prices obtained may not be especially low. This is the case when the sellers all have unique solutions for which there are no direct competitors, and even more so when the bidders' backlogs are so large that they do not need to scrabble for additional business.

> **Tip:** Do not allow a supplier to provide portions (or all) of the requirements text for an RFP, since they will slant the requirements to favor their offerings. Canny competitors will spot this, realize that the RFP requirements have been skewed to favor one seller, and back out of the bidding.

Another way to solicit proposals is to pursue a *sole source* arrangement. This is the best alternative when there is not enough time to pursue the competitive bidding option, or when the total cost is low enough that the savings to be gained from competitive bidding would be immaterial. Sole sourcing may also make sense when the buyer is more concerned with obtaining high-quality service, or wants a project to be completed within a compressed time schedule. Companies routinely take this approach when they have been dealing with the same supplier for an extended period of time and are comfortable with the relationship.

When making the decision to sole source, the contract manager should consider whether it will still be possible to obtain a reasonable price from a supplier that knows there is no other bidder. Also, it may still be useful to conduct a survey of the offerings of other suppliers, to ensure that the buyer will still be receiving the right solution for its needs by sticking with the selected supplier. Another consideration is whether to insist on a high degree of costing transparency from the selected supplier, in order to gain some insight into whether the supplier is inflating its prices.

> **Tip:** When sole sourcing, it is still necessary to provide the selected supplier with a detailed scope of work, as would be prepared for a competitive bidding situation. Doing so reduces the risk of deliverable problems and cost overruns because of the supplier's uncertain understanding of what the buyer wants from it.

A third way to solicit proposals is a *reverse auction*. In this arrangement, the buyer puts up a request on an Internet-based reverse auctioning site for a required good or service, and sellers anonymously place bids for the amount they are willing to be paid; at the end of the auction, the seller with the lowest amount wins. During the process, the sellers can see the current low bid, but not the name of the party that has submitted it. Each seller can submit a series of bids if it wants to beat the currently-posted lowest bid price. For this process to succeed, the buyer has to issue a detailed RFP, so that the sellers have sufficient detail about what the buyer wants. Depending on the Internet platform used, the sellers can send questions back to the buyer, typically to request clarification about the RFP requirements.

Reverse auctions are most useful when the goods or services to be purchased are highly standardized, so that there is little to differentiate between the offerings of the bidders. At the end of the process, the buyer will likely have obtained the lowest possible price. However, there is a risk that the winning seller will give the buyer's order a low priority in its shipping queue, since the seller is probably generating quite a low profit on the transaction. Low supplier loyalty is a particular problem in reverse auction situations, since they must continue to bid the lowest possible price in subsequent auctions in order to continue to sell to the buyer.

Constructing an RFP

An RFP can contain many sections, depending on the complexity of the underlying project. The following topics are most commonly found in this document:

- *Scope of work*. This is the single most essential requirement of an RFP, since a poorly-defined scope of work is one of the primary causes of project failure and leads to a large number of expensive change orders. It describes what the buyer expects the seller to do, identifies any work other sellers will be performing that could impact the work, and notes whether the seller will need to provide any equipment as part of its activities. An RFP usually includes an abbreviated scope of work in the executive summary section, and a more detailed statement in a later section.

- *Optional work*. The RFP may include optional work that could be awarded to the successful bidder. If so, the RFP should clearly state that this work is not to be included in the base price submitted in each bidder's proposal. Instead, if the buyer selects the optional work, it will issue a change order that incorporates the option.

- *Technical specifications*. The technical specifications associated with a project (including all drawings) may be substantial, and could be attached as an addendum to the RFP. If these specifications are altered during the RFP process, then all active bidders must be notified of the changes. To ensure that all changes are properly identified, a revision number and revision date should be attached to each set of specifications.

- *Quality standards*. The RFP should state the quality standards to which a successful bidder will be held. If the bidder will be allowed to use its own quality assurance programs to meet these standards, then the RFP should state whether the buyer reserves the right to review these programs. The buyer may need to state that penalties will be imposed when there are significant defects in the delivered product that require rework.

- *Special requirements*. Any special requirements should be clearly identified in the RFP. For example, it could identify any high-risk activity that could cause injuries or property damage, or the handling or disposal of hazardous waste.

- *Administrative procedures*. The RFP should reference any buyer procedures with which a seller must comply. These procedures can cover a broad range of topics, including the proper sourcing of materials to ensure that they are in compliance with all environmental standards, and ensuring that all local labor laws are met during the construction of a building.

- *Permits and licenses*. If the RFP relates to a construction project, then it should identify all permits and licenses that will be required for the work. Any permits and licenses already held by the buyer should be identified.

- *Staffing*. If the work involves consulting activities, the RFP can mandate that each bidder supply the names of all key personnel who will be assigned to the project, stating their experience and relevant qualifications, as well as the proportion of their time that will be assigned to the buyer.

- *Subcontractors.* If a bidder plans to use subcontractors, the RFP can mandate that these subcontractors be listed in the bidder's response package, along with their experience with the work to be assigned to them. This list can include a description of the work that will be assigned to each subcontractor, as well as its contact information. Another possibility is to require the bidder to describe its experience working with these subcontractors on similar projects.
- *Environmental responsibilities.* The RFP should state whether the seller is responsible for any environmental risks or hazardous wastes arising from the project, and how these issues are to be dealt with. This is a particular concern when the seller is expected to be working on the premises of the buyer.
- *Clean up.* If work is to be conducted on the premises of the buyer, then the RFP should state how the site will be cleaned up and waste disposed of once the work has been completed. In addition, if any of the scrap has value, the RFP should state who will own it.
- *Seller liabilities.* If the seller will be using buyer-provided materials or equipment, the RFP should state the seller's liabilities if these items are damaged or destroyed during the work. For example, when the buyer is providing an air conditioning unit to a contractor as part of a construction project, the contractor will be liable if the unit is damaged during the installation process.
- *Incentives.* If a seller can lower the costs of the buyer or increase value in some other way, then the RFP should state the nature of any incentives that will be built into the contract. It is not recommended to add incentives when there is no offsetting benefit for the buyer.
- *Damages.* If the buyer's intent is to state in the final contract that time is of the essence in completing a contract, then it will have a legal right to impose damages on the seller if it does not complete the designated work by the stated due date. If so, it makes sense to list in the RFP all damages that the buyer intends to impose for an extended completion date. When a "time is of the essence" clause will be inserted into a contract, one can expect that bidders will increase their quoted prices (perhaps substantially) in order to pour resources into the work, thereby avoiding any damages.

  Damages can also be imposed when there is a financial cost to the buyer resulting from the actions of the seller or the seller's failure to act. The relevant damages clause could state that damages will be deducted from seller billings in the amount of any rework, repairs, insurance deductibles, clean-up charges, or fines.
- *Payment structure.* The RFP can include the structure of the payment schedule that the buyer intends to use, such as a certain percentage of the total amount up-front for custom work, or a certain percentage withheld until after the work has been reviewed and approved. For longer-duration projects, the RFP may state the time intervals or milestones at which payments will be made.

- *Economies of scale.* When there is a possibility that the buyer may purchase a large number of units over a period of time, the RFP can state that the buyer expects a price decrease as additional tranches of units are ordered. Doing so allows the buyer to share in any economies of scale experienced by the seller. For example, an RFP to buy 1,000 laptop computers can specify a 5% price drop for any additional purchases of laptops until 5,000 units are acquired, after which an 8% price drop is expected.
- *Cost reimbursements.* When a contract is going to be based on a cost-reimbursement model, the RFP must state exactly which costs will be reimbursed, as well as the mark-ups that the seller can apply to these costs. In addition, clearly define all costs that will *not* be reimbursed, so that there will be no arguments about these items later.
- *Unit price estimates.* There may be cases in which the scope of work can be clearly defined, but not the total quantity of work. Bidders cannot realistically estimate the total price unless they have some idea of the total number of units that will be purchased, so the buyer should state a unit quantity that is reasonably close to its purchasing expectations. If the actual number of units purchased varies substantially from this estimate, then the buyer should allow the seller to adjust its per-unit pricing to more closely relate its costs incurred to payments received from the buyer. For example, if the military issues an RFP for a new fighter jet with an expected purchase quantity of 500 jets, it should allow the successful bidder to adjust its per-unit price if the number of jets purchased actually turns out to be less than 450.
- *Performance bond.* State whether a performance bond will be required to ensure that a project is satisfactorily completed. Be aware that the cost of this bond may prevent smaller and less liquid prospective sellers from submitting a bid.
- *Instructions for submitting a proposal response.* The RFP should state the number of proposal response copies to be submitted, whether an electronic version shall also be submitted, how the submission envelope shall be addressed, whether a table of conformance must be included (stating whether all requirements have been met), whether all areas of non-conformance are to be identified, the submission date, and the location at which the proposal response must be received.
- *RFP schedule.* The RFP should state the dates on which each step in the RFP process is to be accomplished, including the dates of any bidder information meetings and the date by which an award date is expected.
- *Proposal evaluation criteria.* There should be clear criteria for how bidder proposals will be evaluated, usually with a maximum point score that will be assigned to each evaluation area.
- *Confirmation of receipt notice.* This is a standard form, on which an RFP recipient states that the RFP package has been received, and that it will or will not submit a bid. This information is useful for monitoring the number of proposals that are likely to be received.

Tip: All revisions made to the technical specifications and drawings associated with an RFP should be referenced in the final contract, so that the seller will be liable to fulfill the most recent set of specifications. Otherwise, the buyer will be liable for the cost of any additional work by the seller to conform to the latest changes in specifications.

Tip: When providing notice of incentives to bidders in an RFP, be sure to carefully define what conditions will trigger these incentives and how they will be calculated. Otherwise, the buyer may eventually find itself in contentious discussions about whether an incentive has been earned, and its amount. The use of an example within the RFP can clarify how and when an incentive would be calculated and paid.

As noted in one of the preceding bullet points, bidders will likely need to submit a *table of conformance*. This is a listing of every requirement set forth by the buyer, with a notation next to it regarding whether the bidder's offering will meet the requirement. The bidder may note whether its solution fully meets the requirement, partially, only with customization, or not at all. The buyer may also mandate that the bidder's responses include a page reference in its proposal, so that reviewers can more easily find the relevant background information.

Preparing the contents of an RFP can require a substantial effort, to the point where it is quite likely to fail or at least be issued with significant problems unless the buyer fully staffs an RFP development team sufficiently far in advance of the RFP release date to ensure that it has been thoroughly assembled and reviewed. Some of the team members will need to be retained after the RFP has been released, in order to respond to requests for information from bidders.

The contract manager might not directly write any part of an RFP. Writing the RFP, and especially the scope of work, should be assigned to those people most directly involved in the underlying work. For example, the project engineers and architects involved in the design of a new corporate headquarters building are best placed to write the scope of work for an RFP that is being issued to contractors who are bidding to build the structure. The contract manager's role is to ensure that the final RFP document properly addresses all necessary topics.

Locating Suppliers

Given the large amount of money to be awarded under a bid contract, one must be particularly careful in vetting the suppliers who will receive a bid package. One option is to drop from consideration all suppliers who have been awarded work by the buyer in the past, and received failing-to-average scores for their work. These scores may be based on late project completion dates, cost overruns, poor work quality, and so forth. Whatever the reason may be, it is useful to have a process in place for recording the outcomes of completed projects, along with their associated scores, and referring back to it when compiling a list of prospective suppliers for a new contract.

A reverse outcome from having such a database is that one can extract from it those suppliers having previously received outstanding scores. This information can be used to limit the distribution of bid packages to just those suppliers whose prior scores classify them as top-notch suppliers. An expansion of the concept of using these better suppliers for bidding purposes is several rating classifications in the database, which are as follows:

- *Qualified suppliers*. These are suppliers that meet the buyer's minimum threshold criteria to be considered as suppliers, but which have not yet been qualified at a higher level. These suppliers can be contacted regarding lower-level bid packages that do not involve tight specifications, narrow delivery windows, or other more advanced performance criteria.
- *Certified suppliers*. These are suppliers whose processes and methods have been examined and certified by the buyer's quality assurance personnel. Any deliveries from these suppliers can bypass the buyer's normal receiving and inspection processes, and move directly to the production or warehousing areas. This classification of supplier would receive bids related to raw materials and merchandise.
- *Preferred suppliers*. These are suppliers that have proven over time to have superior characteristics, including high-quality products, excellent support, and near-perfect delivery performance. All preferred suppliers are already classified as certified suppliers. There may be a purchasing policy to direct as much business toward these suppliers as possible.

If there is to be a ratings database for suppliers, consider populating the database with additional information, such as supplier office locations, last known billing rates, contact information, and other comments. These additional data elements can prove useful if employees want to search through the database for suppliers and learn more about them.

> **Tip:** If a ratings database is used, expand it to all parts of the company, including other subsidiaries. By doing so, a supplier that has been identified as inadequate will be classified as such for anyone reviewing the database, anywhere in the company. This prevents a poor performer from working for the company again.

The Bidding Process

Once an RFP has been created, the purchasing department manages a tightly-choreographed bidding process. This process is intended to conclude the bidding process within a reasonable period of time, while also treating all participants in a fair and equitable manner. The process flow may include the following steps:

1. *Pre-bid conference*. A notice is issued to all suppliers likely to be interested, stating a time and place at which a pre-bid conference will be held. This meeting is used to go over the specifications and bidding requirements, as well as to discuss any other issues with the members of the buyer's bidding team. Attendance may be mandatory – if so, this conference acts as an automatic gate for reducing the number of participating suppliers. A pre-bid conference

is time-consuming for all parties, and so is generally avoided unless the requirements of an RFP are unusually complex.

2. *RFP issuance*. The RFP is issued to all suppliers that have indicated an interest in receiving the documentation.

3. *Response receipts*. Those suppliers choosing to participate submit their proposals to the purchasing department. Their responses are logged in, so there is an official record of receipt.

4. *Bid opening*. No further bids are allowed after the predetermined bid closing date has passed. Shortly thereafter, all bids are opened, and their key contents are transferred to a summary sheet.

5. *Bid evaluation*. The detailed information from each bid is transferred into a summary comparison sheet, where the answers provided by bidders are scored and multiplied by a weighting factor for each answer or aggregation of answers given. Based on the weighted results, a winning bidder is chosen.

6. *Contract creation*. The winning bidder is contacted, and the parties mutually craft a contract that is based on the terms stated in the successful bid.

Any unsolicited proposals received by the buyer should be returned to the bidder. The reason is that these proposals are not based on the RFP, and so may not align with the scope specified in the RFP. This means that the pricing, goods and services stated in an unsolicited proposal will probably not be comparable to those submitted by other bidders. Also, these proposals do not match the submission criteria stated in the RFP, and so are more difficult to evaluate.

There are many consulting firms that provide companies with bid construction and evaluation services. They have templates of possible requirements, which are then refined during meetings with buyer employees. The consultants can develop a complete RFP, and provide additional support during the bid evaluation process, including compiling scores for all successful bids. Their job is not to select a supplier for a buyer, but rather to facilitate the process.

Handling Inquiries

Even the best RFP will include phrases that are unclear, have terms that are not defined, or do not address certain topics at a sufficient level of detail. This means that suppliers actively interested in responding to the RFP will likely make inquiries on certain points. When the purchasing department receives one of these inquiries, it records the date and nature of the inquiry, as well as the response made to the bidder. The person managing the RFP document can then choose to either issue a copy of this correspondence to all of the bidders whenever such an inquiry is made, or let them pile up for a short time and then issue a consolidated notice. It is important to ensure that all parties receive the responses to all inquiries made – otherwise, those bidders that have obtained points of clarification can use these clarifications to their advantage in preparing their bids.

RFP Confidentiality

The confidentiality of information is crucial to the proper administration of an RFP. If any information leaks out to one bidder and not the others, it gives that bidder an advantage over its competitors, so that the bidding process is no longer fair. A further concern is that the release of confidential information damages the reputation of the buyer, since it will be perceived as administering a rigged RFP process that favors a specific bidder. This can result in fewer participants in the buyer's next RFP process.

The best way to deal with a confidentiality issue is to accumulate all requests for information from bidders and then distribute both these questions and the buyer's answers to all of the bidders. In addition, the buyer should mandate that all requests for information from bidders be channeled to one person at the buyer, who controls the flow of information. In the absence of such a designated person, it is more likely that bidder requests will be sprayed amongst a number of people at the buyer, potentially resulting in the distribution of confidential information. To ensure that information is tightly controlled, the buyer will need to promulgate a policy concerning this issue.

Confidentiality also applies to the receipt of proposals from bidders. When the buyer receives a proposal, it should be sealed in a secure location until a formal bid opening meeting, which should always be witnessed by a manager from the purchasing department. This level of confidentiality is needed to deter any subsequent accusations of bid tampering.

Confidentiality needs to be extended through the *entire* RFP process, until the point at which a contract has been signed with the party submitting the winning bid. This means that *no* qualified bidder should be informed that it has lost until a contract has been signed with the winner, on the grounds that it may not be possible to arrive at an acceptable contract with the winning bidder. If so, the buyer will need to conduct contract negotiations with its second or even third choice. If secrecy is not maintained in this area and no deal can be arranged with the top-rated bidder, then the lower-ranked bidders will know that they can now strike a more favorable deal, given the absence of a key competitor from the bidding.

Evaluating an RFP Response

The evaluation of proposals begins with an analysis to see if each proposal meets the general criteria set by the buyer. If a proposal was not submitted in accordance with the RFP instructions and/or does not provide a complete response to all RFP questions, then it will be rejected. This preliminary analysis can be conducted by referring to a checklist of what needs to be included in a proposal. Also, if a bidder does not have the financial resources, staffing, skills, or integrity to perform the required work, then its proposal will be rejected. This requires a more detailed review by the buyer's evaluation team. All remaining bidders are classified as qualified bidders, and can proceed to a more detailed evaluation of the technical and commercial aspects of their proposals.

> **Tip:** Any bidders that do not pass the buyer's threshold criteria can be notified at once that their bids have been rejected, along with a brief summary of the reasons for rejection and a thank you note for having participated in the process.

The proposals of all remaining bidders are subjected to a two-part review process. A technical review team evaluates whether a bidder's experience, technical expertise, staffing, and work schedule will be sufficient to complete the work needed by the buyer. This analysis may include site visits to the facilities of the bidder, and possibly to the facilities of selected customer locations where its products are being used. The team will also produce a risk analysis that identifies any areas in which a bidder would be at risk of experiencing technical difficulties or not delivering by the mandated due date. This group also determines whether there are any issues in the following areas:

- Whether the bidder is using proven technology
- Whether the bidder meets the buyer's information security standards
- Whether the bidder is already working on other projects that could compete with this project
- Whether the bidder will need to subcontract key parts of the proposed work
- Whether the bidder has detailed oversight of the work of its subcontractors
- Whether a large part of the bidder's proposed staff have recently been hired
- Whether the bidder has an effective safety program
- Whether the bidder can increase crew sizes to maintain its schedule

In addition, a commercial review team evaluates whether a bidder's price and related incentives and damages are competitive in relation to the same information submitted by other bidders. For a really detailed analysis, the review team may want to compare the price breakdown submitted by each bidder, to see if there are any anomalies hidden within the total price figure that should be clarified with the bidders. This group also determines whether there are any issues in the following areas:

- Whether the bidder is experiencing any financial difficulties
- Whether the bidder is involved in any legal actions
- Whether the bidder has sufficient bonding capacity
- Whether the bidder has sufficient insurance coverage
- Whether the bidder has reasonable relations with its unions
- Whether the bidder's employee turnover level is reasonable

This commercial review team is particularly concerned with the investigation of any submitted prices that seem inordinately low, to see if the bidder understood the nature of the work to be performed and properly calculated its bid. Though the buyer might be able to force an inordinately low bidder to perform at its quoted price, this may result in significant problems, so it is better to identify and set aside bids containing pricing errors.

> **Tip:** When the submitted bid prices are widely scattered, this is an indicator that the scope included in an RFP was either vague or incomplete.

During their work, the technical and commercial review teams may have questions for bidders regarding their proposals. If so, all questions should be routed in writing through the contract manager, who passes them along to the bidders. The return information flow from the bidders also goes through the contract manager. This regimented approach is needed to maintain control over the confidentiality of information.

There are several best practices that the RFP review teams can use. Consider focusing on the following items:

- *Independent evaluations.* When the buyer wants to achieve the highest possible level of objectivity in evaluating proposals, several people can be asked to independently score the same proposals. One can then review these scores for consistency, and average them to arrive at a final score.
- *Bidder references.* For the more expensive contracts, it can make sense to send an evaluation team to a bidder's customer references. Doing so gives the review teams a more detailed view of how well a bidder has supported its customers and continues to interact with them. These references may provide the names of the customers of a bidder who were not included as references; talking to these additional parties may provide a more nuanced view of a bidder's capabilities.
- *Front end loading.* The buyer should watch out for proposed payment terms that pay the seller a large part of the total price up-front, where the seller is not incurring roughly the same costs through that period. When this is the case, the seller has essentially earned a portion of its profit before the work is complete, and so gives it less incentive to do a thorough job of completing the work. A good way to detect front-end loading in an RFP response is to compare the proposed pricing schedules of all bidders. Any large disparity in proposed payments will stand out when this comparison is made.
- *Government pricing availability.* When a bidder has previously sold goods and services to a government entity, there is a good chance that the prices at which these contracts were concluded is publicly available. If so, it can be useful to obtain this information, to see how a bidder's prices compare to its previous deals with other customers. Similarly, pricing information may be located in court documents from previous lawsuits, which can be made available upon request.
- *Pricing schedule.* If the buyer has required bidders to break down their prices by each phase of a longer-term project, it can be useful to compare the submitted prices by all bidders for each phase of the work. This analysis can highlight instances in which a bidder may have incorrectly formulated a price, based on a pricing spike or drop in comparison to the group average.
- *Incentive proposals.* When a bidder inserts an incentive clause in its bid, be sure to question how the buyer will receive value from the performance criteria that the bidder has proposed. For example, it does not make sense to agree

to an incentive for delivering a parking lot two weeks early when the office building to which it will be adjacent will not yet be operational.

> **Tip:** Never agree to an incentive payment that is tied to a seller meeting an interim milestone, since doing so does not ensure that the overall project will be a success once it has been completed. In particular, never agree to an incentive to cut short the scoping and conceptual engineering phase of a project, since this is an iterative process that must be thoroughly addressed in order to shorten the duration of all subsequent tasks.

Once the technical and commercial reviews have been completed, they are brought together into a final analysis, to determine the best value amongst the remaining bidders. This is done by ranking the bidders from the scores derived by the two review teams. A best value bidder should be the party that has both the capacity and capability to properly complete the scope of work specified by the buyer, can do so at a reasonable cost, and has a high probability of completing the work.

> **Tip:** When the technical and commercial review teams will require a substantial amount of time to review each submitted proposal, it makes sense to increase the rigor of the initial review process, so that fewer bidders pass the initial qualification threshold.

The scoring system used to rank bidder proposals should be clearly defined, so that there is no question about how to assign a score to each proposal. Doing so puts the emphasis on a highly quantified outcome, rather than one that is derived primarily from qualitative opinions. An example of the definitions used for a zero-to-five scoring system appears in the following exhibit.

Sample Scoring Definitions

Score	Definition
0	The bidder's proposal has a significant fault that is unacceptable to the buyer, and which cannot be corrected. This will result in a near-certain scheduling delay or inadequate performance level.
1	The bidder's proposal has a borderline unacceptable fault that will be difficult to cure. Additional effort and cost will be required to bring the issue up to an acceptable level. This presents a high risk of a scheduling delay or inadequate performance.
2	The bidder's proposal is satisfactory, but contains problems that will need some corrective effort or added resources to ensure that performance levels are acceptable. This presents a modest risk of a scheduling delay or inadequate performance.
3	The bidder's proposal is largely acceptable, and it is probable that the bidder will be able to perform at an acceptable level. This presents a low risk of a scheduling delay or inadequate performance.

Score	Definition
4	The bidder's proposal is completely acceptable, and various bidder attributes make it a superior bidder. The bidder will not require any additional oversight or support from the buyer. This presents a low risk of a scheduling delay or inadequate performance.
5	The bidder's proposal is completely acceptable, and various attributes give it a clear advantage over the other bidders. This presents a high probability of enhanced bidder performance.

Handling Complaints

From time to time, a bidder may protest the outcome of a bidding situation. Perhaps the supplier feels that certain aspects of its proposal were not fully considered, or perhaps there is a suspicion that the outcome was skewed. Whatever the reason for the complaint, the purchasing department should have a procedure in place for dealing with it in a standardized manner. This usually encompasses the following steps:

1. *Provide a written complaint.* Have the bidder write down its complaint, stating the nature of the issue, and attaching any relevant supporting documentation. This is an improvement over a verbal complaint, where the nature of the issue may be subject to interpretation.
2. *Formal log-in.* Each complaint is logged in, so there is a record of receipt. Otherwise, there is a risk of a complaint being "lost" within the organization and not being dealt with.
3. *Review by separate committee.* A group of senior staff and managers meets periodically to review all bidder complaints. This group should not include anyone directly involved with the RFP under review, to keep from skewing the results of the group's findings. This committee is empowered to conduct its own investigation and issue rulings.
4. *Issue response.* Any bidder that has taken the trouble to formally protest an award should certainly be given the dignity of a response. Consequently, the review committee should write a response to every bidder, stating its reasons for or against the original award.

If an award has been made by a government entity, bidders routinely file complaints regarding contract awards. These complaints are much less frequent when an award has been issued by a buyer – perhaps because bidders are aware that a frequent complainer will not be included in future bidding processes. In the latter case, an aggrieved bidder will probably just stop submitting bids if it does not believe it is being dealt with fairly.

Contract Negotiations

Once a bidder has been selected, it will still be necessary to conduct contract negotiations. This is because the bidder wants to change some of the terms stated in the RFP, or because the scope encompassed by the contract is somewhat different from the scope stated in the RFP. In these negotiations, the buyer should always maintain a backup bidder (or two), in case there is a breakdown in the negotiations with the selected bidder. This gives the buyer leverage over the bidder, since there will always be a backup party available.

Tip: A good reason not to sole source a contract is that the bidder knows there is no alternative bidder on which the buyer can rely, so the bidder can drive a harder bargain during contract negotiations.

A potential area of conflict arises when the buyer wants to pare back some aspects of the original scope of work. When this happens, the seller will want to reallocate a portion of its overhead to the remaining work to be conducted. This means that the seller will want to increase the price of the remaining work to incorporate the additional overhead charge. This can come as a surprise to the buyer, who might have expected a larger cost reduction when it reduced the scope of work.

The reverse situation can also arise, where the buyer wants to add to the scope of a project. This may arise when the buyer's evaluation of a seller indicates that it is a high-quality entity with superior capabilities. However, an issue to watch out for is when the scope is expanded into an area with which the seller is less familiar. When this is the case, it is quite possible that the seller's weaker capabilities in this added area result in a significantly reduced outcome. Consequently, it can make sense to ask for a seller's honest opinion of its capabilities in out-of-scope areas, to see if it really makes sense to assign additional work to the seller.

Contract Approval Process

The amount of time spent reviewing and approving contracts with suppliers should strike a balance between the risk of allowing unfavorable terms, the time required to complete a review, and the delay that a review introduces into the process of obtaining goods and services. The general guideline for contract approvals is that the purchasing staff is assigned a monetary threshold, below which no additional approvals are required. If a staff person has considerable experience, the approval threshold might be raised to a higher level. Above this threshold, the approval of the purchasing manager might be needed, as long as the standard terms and conditions are used in the contract. If the contract amount both exceeds the review threshold *and* contains altered terms and conditions, then the legal staff must also review and approve the document. This approval process flow focuses attention on those contracts that could potentially result in unusually high expenditures for the buyer.

Contract Clauses

We already dealt with contract terms and conditions in the *Contract Terms and Conditions* chapter. In this section, we only note a few contract clauses that should be a particular focus of negotiation for the contract manager, as they can have a particular impact on the cost of a contract or the effort required to complete it.

Responsibility Clause

The responsibility clause states that the seller is solely responsible for the goods to be delivered and services to be performed. The seller may attempt to split responsibility with another contractor, but this can cause problems with blame shifting in the event of a failure. Therefore, the buyer should designate a lead contractor who takes full responsibility for the work.

Damages Clause

The damages clause identifies the circumstances under which penalties will be imposed on the seller, as well as how those damages are calculated. The clause may address several types of damages, which were described in Chapter 1. Most sellers will want the buyer to limit or waive the damages clause, so this area can be a point of contention between the parties.

A particular concern for the buyer is to set the amount of liquidated damages in a contract at a reasonable level that approximates the amount of damages that would actually be incurred. Otherwise, a court might find that large damages are unenforceable, on the grounds that they constitute a punishment for a breach, rather than reimbursement for damages incurred.

Payment Schedule

It is not useful for a buyer to force a seller to go into a negative cash position during a project, since the interest costs that the seller must incur to fund the work will be passed through to the buyer. A better approach is to structure a payment schedule that covers the costs of the seller throughout the term of the contract.

Options Clause

An options clause states the price at which the buyer can obtain optional work from the seller, as well as the date by which this order must be placed. Past that date, the parties will have to renegotiate the price of the optional work.

Contractual Disputes

Over time, contract managers are likely to be involved in any number of contractual disputes. They might be caused by the fundamental intransigence of the parties to a contract, but it is also possible that a dispute hinges on the interpretation of a contract clause, or someone's opinion of the goods or services being provided. If so, it is possible that settlement of a dispute will require an inordinate amount of time and money, as the parties establish their positions and debate points of law in court. There are alternative ways to settle disputes that can keep a buyer and its suppliers out of the courtroom. These alternatives also allow for a greater degree of privacy, rather than the public forum of a courtroom dispute. The alternatives are as follows:

- *Mediation.* The parties jointly hire a mediator, whose task is to work with both sides to arrive at a compromise position. The parties do not have to accept a solution suggested by the mediator.
- *Arbitration.* The parties agree to allow a third party to examine the facts of the dispute, and make a ruling that both parties agree in advance to accept (known as binding arbitration). This arrangement is relatively inexpensive and can be completed quickly.
- *Rent-a-judge.* A court refers a pending lawsuit to a neutral third party, who conducts what is essentially a private trial. The third party, who may be a retired judge, then renders an opinion, which the parties may or may not accept.

The choice to use mediation and/or arbitration should be built into each contract. This clause describes the situations in which these methods can be used, and the method by which the parties will agree on a mediator or arbitrator. The rent-a-judge option does not appear in contracts, since this is essentially a referral from the court system.

A potentially significant issue to address in a contract if the parties are located far apart is where hearings will be held. Since it may be necessary for several people to travel to a mediator or arbitrator more than once, this can be a moderately expensive proposition for the more distant of the two parties.

Summary

An RFP is the basis for a bidding process that is intended to locate a best value bidder. For an RFP process to work properly, the contract manager must ensure that a thoroughly compiled and reviewed RFP is issued, that all interactions with bidders are conducted properly, and that a clearly-defined process is used to evaluate submitted bids. Otherwise, a buyer may find itself saddled with a supplier that does not have the financial or technical resources to complete the required work within a reasonable period of time.

Chapter 5
Project Preparation

Introduction

Once a contract has been signed with the winning bidder, there is a preparation period before the seller begins work or delivers the mandated goods or services. This involves a significant amount of planning coordination between the parties to ensure that the seller's work is properly installed (in the case of fixed assets) or incorporated into processes (in the case of services). In this chapter, we cover how project preparation is to be managed.

Project Preparation

It is much more important for the buyer that a contract be completed properly than it is for the seller (who will only suffer from a bad reference), so the contract manager has to be particularly attentive to all aspects of project preparation after a contract with a seller has been signed. This means that the contract manager will need to be heavily involved in all four of the steps outlined in the following sub-sections.

Step 1: Work Preplanning

Depending on the type of project, the buyer may need to make services available to support the seller, including use of the buyer's existing infrastructure. It may even be necessary to construct facilities for the seller. Examples of the infrastructure that may be required include office space, shop space, and warehouse storage, as well as temporary water and electrical lines, temporary toilets, and access roads. Furthermore, the buyer may need to obtain permits for the seller to transport oversized loads and hazardous materials to a work site on the buyer's premises.

> **Tip:** Identify in advance all permits that will not be issued without the appropriate engineering documents, and estimate the resources required to develop those documents.

The buyer may also need to inspect the seller's planning documentation, which may include a project plan, quality assurance plan, environmental plan, budget, and staffing plan. The buyer's inspection is targeted at ensuring that the seller's documentation fully reflects the work to be completed. In order to review these documents, the buyer needs to have the correct skill set on staff to understand the nature of the seller's documentation and determine whether it is complete in all respects.

Tip: A contract should state that the buyer will review and provide comments on documents submitted to it by the seller, and not that the buyer approves these documents. This wording allows the buyer to avoid responsibility for the seller's documents.

A key part of the contract manager's monitoring process is determining whether the seller has actually assigned those people to the job who were originally scheduled for it in the proposal document. An additional concern to investigate is whether the general experience level of the people assigned to the work is adequate for the tasks associated with the project. This is an essential activity, since some sellers make a habit of including their most experienced people in proposal documents, and then substituting in less experienced people after winning a contract.

Tip: The contract manager should closely monitor any activities or purchases by the seller that involve long lead times, in order to be fully warned of any situations in which a delay in one of these areas could imperil the projected project completion date.

Step 2: Deployment Planning

Depending on the type of project, the buyer may need to take a hand in the planning for the deployment of the seller's personnel to the buyer's premises. This may include such activities as the investigation of personnel for security clearances, drug screenings, safety orientations, and training in how to move about in the buyer's facilities. This will require some coordination with the seller, to ensure that the buyer's deployment planning staff is not overwhelmed with a large number of applicants all at once. An additional concern is coordinating the replacement of seller staff with the seller's administrative team when someone does not pass the buyer's screening process.

Tip: The contract manager should be particularly attentive to this stage, because any delay in the deployment of seller personnel can result in claims of buyer-caused delays, which can increase the amount billed to the buyer.

A variation on the concept is for the contract manager to certify the seller to engage in all or most of the aforementioned deployment activities. This approach is most useful when the seller is going to deploy a large number of staff, perhaps cycling through replacements on a regular basis. In this case, the seller takes full responsibility for all deployment activities.

Tip: The contract manager should ensure that the engineering related to a construction project has been sufficiently completed to warrant the deployment of personnel to the job site; otherwise, the seller will incur extra costs when construction has to be redone as engineering plans are revised.

Deployment planning also includes flagging the work area for site entrance and egress points, as well as any high risk or high security areas, allowed parking areas, and the locations of any buried cabling or pipes. If there are any environmentally sensitive areas, then they should be prominently indicated. If the seller will be building facilities on-site, then lay out the areas in which these facilities will be located.

A further planning concept is setting up areas in which to store and dispose of hazardous materials. This can include setting up a reporting process for any instances in which hazardous materials are spilled.

When a major construction project is contemplated, the contract manager may need to coordinate planned activities with local government employees, such as the department of transportation, the police department, and the department of public works, since the project may impact these entities.

Step 3: Seller Monitoring Planning

Depending on the type of project, both the buyer and seller will create policies, procedures, and controls to monitor activities. These actions are taken to ensure that both parties have a progress reporting system in place, as well as a budget review system to ensure that activities and costs incurred are being closely monitored. The reporting that the buyer wants to see should be included in the contract as reporting requirements; seller monitoring planning is designed to delve into the details of exactly what these reports must contain.

Step 4: Contract Administration Planning

Depending on the type of project, the contract manager will need to develop a system for monitoring how well the seller is adhering to its schedule, and how well it is adhering to its budget. In addition, the manager may need to develop systems to monitor the quality levels of the seller. Based on these outcomes, the manager's team will then need a system to determine the amount of any periodic payments to be made to the seller. The payment system will vary, depending on the type of contract that the buyer has with the seller. These systems are noted in the following bullet points:

- *Cost-reimbursement contract.* In this arrangement, the seller submits an invoice that is compiled from its hours worked, materials purchased, and equipment rented. The contract manager's team will need to verify that the supporting documents submitted along with the invoice substantiate the amount billed. This can be a massive verification job for a larger contract, so team members may sample just a portion of the total amount of supporting documents in order to gain assurance that the total billed amount is reasonable.
- *Fixed price contract.* In this arrangement, the seller will invoice when each milestone or target date is reached, while the buyer will want to ensure that the full value associated with making each payment has been achieved before issuing payment. This usually means investigating the claimed percentage of completion to verify that it has indeed been achieved, and discussing with the seller any situations in which this does not appear to be the case. It may be necessary to examine the seller costs associated with work activities at a fine-grained level, to ensure that the seller has in fact incurred the costs associated

with those specific work activities. A key issue in making these determinations is that the seller is kept in a cash-neutral position in regard to the contract, so that it is not put in a position of having a serious cash shortfall that could impair its ability to complete the contract.

- *Unit price contract.* In this arrangement, the seller submits an invoice that states the number of units delivered. The contract manager's team will need to verify how the unit counts and unit prices are determined. There may be several technical issues involved in these determinations. For example, payments made to move soil will depend on the extent to which it has been compacted; unit prices will vary, based on the density of the material.

Summary

Taking the time to prepare for the beginning of a project can reap substantial rewards for the contract manager, because it increases the odds that the seller will seamlessly start work when expected, with the correct resources in place. This requires a substantial amount of interaction with the seller, to ensure that the correct personnel are being deployed, that all permits are in place, and that the supporting policies and procedures have been correctly designed and installed.

Chapter 6
Monitoring Contract Performance

Introduction

When a seller is performing the work and making deliveries as mandated under the terms of a signed contract, the contract manager should undertake those activities needed to be assured that the seller is fulfilling its obligations. An effective contract manager should be able to assure the buyer that work was conducted on schedule, within the agreed-upon budget, and to the specifications stated in the contract. In addition, the processes used by the contract manager should be able to spot any variances in the scheduled completion dates, costs, or quality levels as early as possible, so that corrective actions can be taken. We address these topics in the following pages, along with a discussion of change orders, claims, and back charges.

Necessary Staffing Levels

A buyer does not want to be in the position where the seller starts to experience trouble fulfilling its obligations, and the buyer is the last party to find out about it. This places the buyer in the uncomfortable position of having to scramble to correct the situation, which may include incurring substantial additional costs. To keep this from happening, the contract manager needs to be supported with a sufficiently large team to adequately monitor the work being done, and to spot looming problems with ongoing variance analysis. This also means that the contract manager's team must have enough capacity to work with the seller to remediate problems as they arise.

The exact amount of staffing needed by the contract manager will depend on the type of work. For example, the delivery and installation of goods that have already been manufactured will require substantially fewer internal resources than the monitoring of a large construction crew that will be on-site for several years. The staffing level will also be impacted by the experience of the two parties in dealing with each other in the past. If there is a long-term history of working together, then the probability of being surprised by variances declines, and the contract manager may be able to pare back the amount of staffing assigned to contract monitoring. Conversely, if the seller is a new one, then a prudent contract manager will be more likely to bulk up his or her staff to provide more comprehensive coverage of the activities of the seller.

> **Tip:** It can be useful to develop work assignments for the contract manager's staff based on identified project risks (as described earlier in the Contracting Risks chapter), so that key risk areas are being fully monitored.

Adequate contract management staffing is also needed just to stay ahead of the variety of administrative tasks associated with a contract. These activities include the processing of change orders, the preparation of amendments to the original contract, the completion of audits, and the processing of seller invoices. Minimal staffing for these tasks can result in extra costs for the buyer, quite possibly at a level that greatly exceeds the cost of the associated staffing.

Monitoring Activities

The contract manager's team will need to monitor several items to ensure that the seller is completing work properly. These items include the following:

- Comparison of actual to budgeted work schedule
- Comparison of actual to budgeted staffing levels
- Comparison of actual to budgeted costs incurred
- Differences between actual and contract specifications
- The level of planning detail completed for upcoming work
- Changes in expected arrival dates for long lead-time items

In order to keep up-to-date on these monitoring activities, the contract manager's team should conduct a daily review with their counterparts at the seller, both in regard to current issues and also to discuss events that are expected to occur over the next few days. In addition, these parties should meet to discuss the completion of specific work tasks and milestones, to evaluate the extent to which they have been completed and how well resource usage is tracking against the plan through these dates. It is especially important to monitor progress toward milestones when there are incentive payments tied to these events, so that the contract manager can evaluate how likely it is that the additional payments will be made.

High-Risk Activities

When there are high-risk activities included in a project, the project manager should be concerned with how well the seller has designed the associated work to minimize the risk. Accordingly, there should be a higher-than-usual level of oversight of the seller's planning for these activities. This may include training on a mock-up of the actual activity, as well as a discussion of the types of safety procedures that will need to be followed. There are many types of high-risk activities, such as activities that could shut down plant operations, the movement of oversized containers, the use of heavy lifts, the use of flammable materials, and work in confined spaces.

The planning for high-risk activities should include a backup plan, in case the work being performed by the seller fails. This can involve having the seller devise a backup plan, or working with a third party to provide the needed service. The latter case may be needed when an initial review of the activity reveals that the seller is at high risk of failure; in this case, using another party with a higher level of expertise is likely to be the preferred solution.

Contract Amendments

The monitoring activities just described are all based on a comparison of actual results to the baseline schedule that the seller agreed to in its contract with the buyer. If the buyer and seller mutually agree that there will be changes to the schedule, this will call for a contract amendment, which will likely alter the baseline schedule. Once an amendment has been agreed upon, the evaluation of seller performance will then be based on the modified baseline schedule, rather than the original one.

> **Tip:** When a contract amendment is made, the contract manager should determine its impact on the critical path of the underlying project, to evaluate how the change impacts the completion date of the work. The *critical path* is the longest path in a project plan. There is no slack in any task on the critical path, so if there is a delay in any of these tasks, the completion of an entire project will be delayed.

Contract Performance Indicators

The contract manager's team should keep close watch over a few indicators of a seller's performance against a contract. In the following sub-sections, we note several possible measures worth considering.

Timeliness of Design Engineering

A likely indicator of the eventual failure of a project is when the detailed design engineering for a project is falling behind. When this happens, the seller is less aware of where its bottlenecks and long lead time items are located, making it more difficult to ensure that the project is completed on time. And in general, delays in this area usually trigger downstream delays in the contracting and construction phases of a project.

Seller Productivity

Comparing the actual hours worked to planned hours can provide an indication of the productivity level of the seller. The buyer should be keenly interested in seller productivity when there is a cost-reimbursement contract, since higher productivity levels will ultimately reduce the seller's billings to the buyer. It is still worthwhile to monitor productivity when there is a fixed price contract, since a low productivity level is a likely indicator that the seller will make change order requests in order to recover lost profits.

In order to compare actual to earned hours, one should calculate the actual and planned hours from the start of a project to a specific date or point on the schedule. When actual hours incurred are less than planned hours, this generally means that the seller's employees are being more productive than planned. However, it can also mean that the seller has skipped or pared back on certain work activities. It will be up to the contract manager's team to find instances in which the latter situation is present.

Tip: If a seller has skipped or pared back on some work activities in order to report a higher productivity level, it may still need to complete these activities later in the project, which means that reported productivity levels will decline towards the end of the project.

The preceding tip points out an issue for the contract manager's team, which is to not just focus on the critical path activities associated with a project. If a seller is not assigning sufficient resources to lower-priority activities within a project, it is entirely possible that these activities will eventually become the new critical path for the project, likely delaying its completion.

Cost to Budget Comparison

A cost to budget comparison is useful for determining whether a seller's costs are running high or low in comparison to the budget. To see if this is the case, the contract manager's team will need to start with a highly-specific budget that assigns costs to even the smaller tasks. It can then accumulate actual costs at a detailed level and match them up to budgeted costs to identify instances of cost overruns.

Tip: If a seller's cost accumulation systems are primitive or not updated on a daily basis, then it can be impossible to make accurate cost to budget comparisons. This issue can be dealt with by specifying how the cost accumulation system should function within the underlying contract.

It is not sufficient to only compare total actual and budgeted costs to date, since a clever seller can easily hide within this gross level of reporting any instances of cost overruns.

Tip: If a project budget has any long-duration activities, it can be difficult to determine if these activities have any cost overruns piling up. To avoid this, chop long-duration activities into a series of smaller ones, and then compare actual to budgeted costs for these shorter intervals.

Change Order Management

When a project involves a fixed fee arrangement, there is a strong likelihood that the scope of the project will change over time. If so, it will be necessary for the seller and buyer to mutually agree upon a change order that specifies the extent of the scope change, as well as the related alteration in the amount that the supplier is now allowed to bill to the buyer. Thus, a *change order* is a document that is used to record an amendment to the original contract. It states the additional services to be provided, as well as the cost of those services.

A change order management process involves a committee that is comprised of the project manager, the contract manager for the buyer, and the project accountant. The project manager and contract manager must approve each change order, while the

71

accountant processes the paperwork for the change order and bills it to the buyer. Various technical personnel from the project team will be brought in to discuss the financial and timing impact of proposed changes to the existing project scope. The committee is also responsible for maintaining the most current listing of project requirements, and for monitoring the project's actual status in comparison to these requirements.

Change requests should be documented on a standardized form, which ensures that the same set of information is provided to the committee whenever a change is proposed. The form should include space for the following information:

- *Change request number.* Needed to uniquely identify each request made. This is useful for ensuring that no requests are lost.
- *Name of the individual requesting the change.* Needed in order to report back the committee's decision, as well as who to contact for more information. This field can include contact information for the requester.
- *Date of the request.* Needed to establish the amount of time that has elapsed before a request is dealt with.
- *Description of the change.* Summarizes the requested change, possibly including an estimate of the impact on project cost, scope, or time of completion.

When the committee receives a change request, it should enter the request into a change order log, so that no forms are inadvertently lost. The log should also state when the committee dealt with each request, and the outcome of that analysis. Once a change order is approved by the committee, the project accountant should enter it into a separate log that is used for billing purposes, to ensure that each change order is billed to the buyer when the related work is completed.

> **Tip:** The contract management team should target a high proportion of change orders for audits, since this is a prime source of profit for sellers. It is common practice for them to inflate charges on change orders through a variety of accounting practices that are worthy of investigation.

Given the high probability of being overcharged for the work conducted under a change order, it makes sense for a contract manager to negotiate a fixed price for the work. If it is not possible to do so, then the contract manager's team should be quite visible in inspecting time sheets and material invoices, so that the seller will understand that its billing practices are being watched.

> **Tip:** The contract manager should issue separate cost codes for each change order, so that the costs associated with each one can be more easily tracked. This prevents a seller from pulling in costs from other parts of a project in order to inflate a change order billing.

The contract manager should have direct oversight over the preparation of all correspondence with the seller regarding change orders, given the large amounts of money that can be involved. This activity should extend to monitoring the progress of each change order, reviews of final seller billings, and closing out each change order to keep additional costs from being charged to the related cost codes.

Disputed Work

There may be cases in which a seller believes that certain work falls outside of the scope of the contract or any subsequent change orders, and therefore claims that an additional change order should be authorized to cover it. The seller documents its position in a claim. A *claim* is a seller notification, stating that it has found a condition not covered by the contract scope, or which interferes with its work. The claim describes the issue, the schedule changes needed to fix the affected work, and the additional work cost of the issue. The seller should deliver a prompt written notice of each claim to the buyer, so that the buyer has adequate time to investigate and possibly mitigate the underlying condition.

Tip: Include in the contract terms and conditions a requirement for the seller to submit claims as expeditiously as possible and in a specific format. Any seller claims that do not comply with this requirement can be voided.

There are many types of issues that can cause a seller to file a claim. Here are some of the more common ones:

- *Accelerated schedule.* The buyer has accelerated the completion due date.
- *Altered sequence.* The buyer has mandated a change in the work sequence that prevents the seller from performing its work as planned.
- *Breach by the buyer.* The buyer has breached the contract requirements, usually involving not making scheduled payments.
- *Changed conditions.* The conditions encountered by the seller differ from what was described by the buyer in the contract.
- *Changed prices.* The seller has encountered unexpected price increases in labor or materials.
- *Changed scope of work.* The buyer has altered the scope of work from what was stated in the contract.
- *Defective specifications.* The specifications provided by the buyer are incorrect.
- *Delays.* The seller cannot conduct work due to a delay caused by the buyer.
- *Poor coordination.* The buyer has failed to coordinate the work between several contractors, causing delays and changed conditions.

The contract manager should address all claims as soon as possible, since they can impact the completion date and cost of a project. The settlement of claims should *not* be delayed, for several reasons. First, members of the contract manager's team who originally dealt with a claims-related issue may roll off the project, so their expertise will not be available to deal with the claims. Second, a delay in payment due to a processing delay could entitle the seller to interest payments. And finally, if claims are not settled until late in a project, a sudden surge in the costs associated with these claims could result in a project suddenly having a large and unexpected negative cost variance.

A common outcome of a claims analysis is the issuance of a change order, as described earlier. However, it is also possible that the contract manager disputes a claim and states that the work is within the existing scope and should proceed. If so, the seller may continue the work under protest, with the intent of filing a claim that may be reviewed by an independent adjudicator. This dispute resolution process should be laid out in the associated contract, stating the documentation that the seller must supply, as well as the use of successive levels of dispute resolution mechanisms, usually culminating in a decision by an independent arbitrator.

When a claim is initially rejected, the contract manager should issue a separate cost code for the work in question, so that its cost can be compiled separately. It is only prudent to do this, so that the actual cost of the work can be accessed in the event that the claim is eventually approved and the seller must be paid. In addition, the contract manager's team should begin to keep notes on all actions taken in relation to the claim, in case this information is needed later as evidence in settlement of the claim.

Tip: The amount of disputed work associated with a project will be reduced when the scope of work is extremely detailed. At a high level of detail, there are fewer areas of work subject to interpretation, from which a claim might arise.

When the contract manager rejects a seller claim, there is a risk that the project will become bogged down as the positions of the parties become increasingly adversarial. When it appears that this is a potential risk, it can make sense to propose a mid-way solution where both parties share a portion of the cost. This is an especially attractive option when a successful project outcome is of great importance to the buyer. If the contract manager is contemplating making a settlement offer, it can be useful to develop a negotiation strategy, on the assumption that there will be some give-and-take between the parties before a final settlement amount is agreed upon.

Back Charges

There are situations in which the contract manager will be responsible for managing claims flowing in the opposite direction – from the buyer to the seller. These claims arise when the seller has not performed its work properly, has damaged the buyer's property, or is found to have overbilled the buyer. In these cases, the contract manager's team investigates the situation, discusses the matter with the seller, and creates a detailed description of the issue. This is known as a *back charge*, which is a demand by the buyer for compensation to offset costs incurred to perform work that the seller should have performed. A back charge may also be filed when the buyer has to obtain materials that should have been supplied by the seller.

Back charges are typically deducted from one of the ongoing payments that the buyer owes to the seller.

Review of Seller Invoices

The review of seller invoices is an essential function of the contract manager, since the seller deserves to be paid promptly for all work that it has properly performed. Conversely, if any of the seller's work products are defective, then the contract manager has an obligation to spot these items and ensure that they are fixed before the associated payment is made.

Since time is of the essence in making payments, the contract manager needs to have sufficient qualified people on staff to verify that the work claimed in an invoice has been correctly completed. This is a particular concern in a cost reimbursement situation, since the buyer has to verify invoiced expenditures, *and* verify that these costs are reimbursable under the terms of the associated contract, *and* verify that the associated work was actually performed. These verification activities are less of a concern for a fixed-price contract, where the main invoice verification task is to ensure that the seller actually performed the indicated work.

The outcome of an invoice verification process may be that not all of the invoice amount will be initially paid. When this is the case, the contract manager should send a message to the seller, itemizing all unpaid amounts and the reasons for nonpayment. A high level of detail is needed in this letter, so that the seller will understand exactly what needs to be done in order to obtain full payment of the invoiced amount.

Summary

Proper monitoring of seller performance is one of the best ways to ensure that a buyer is satisfied with the performance of a seller, since active monitoring makes it more likely that deliverables will be handed over on time and within the expected price point. Further, it behooves the buyer to engage in a significant level of seller oversight, since the buyer will otherwise be burdened by any long-term operational issues or quality concerns related to a deliverable. The contract manager's team is responsible for this monitoring, which involves ongoing reviews of seller work and extensive interactions with the seller's team to discuss and settle claims and back charges.

Chapter 7
Tender and Acceptance

Introduction

When a seller is ready to deliver completed goods or services to the buyer in accordance with contract requirements, the items are said to have been *tendered*. The buyer conducts an inspection at this time, which can result in either the delivery of these items or their rejection due to non-conformance. In this chapter, we cover the concepts of tender and acceptance.

Tender

When a seller issues a notification of tender to a buyer, it is up to the buyer to conduct an inspection to determine whether the goods or services are acceptable. If so, the buyer sends a notification of acceptance to the seller, along with delivery instructions.

As part of the tender process, the buyer reviews all related documentation to ensure that it is complete, and conducts a receipt inspection. This inspection is intended to spot any instances of damage during transit, as well as to see if the delivered items meet all contract requirements. The buyer has a responsibility to perform this inspection as soon as possible.

> **Tip:** Have a different team conduct the receipt inspection than the inspectors who have been conducting inspections of the buyer's work during the construction phase. The use of different parties eliminates the risk of having an excessive degree of familiarity with the work, and therefore not conducting a rigorous receipt inspection.

Inspections may be conducted at the seller's facility. This makes sense when the seller is better-equipped to make corrections in its own shop, rather than at the buyer's location. This means that the buyer will need to send inspection teams off-site, possibly for extended periods of time.

The buyer may elect to use a third-party testing service for some inspections. For example, a specialist could be brought in to inspect welds, while materials tests could be performed by an outside laboratory. Some of these tests may be destructive, in which case the seller will need to provide extra units for the testing.

> **Note:** For large projects, the buyer should have been conducting inspections of the seller's work all along. This means that any issues found during the final inspection should be relatively small. If not, it is possible that the buyer's inspections over the course of the project were inadequate.

If the buyer's inspection results in acceptance, then it has an obligation to render final payment to the seller as stated in the contract terms. Conversely, if the buyer rejects the items, then the contract manager must issue an immediate rejection notice in writing to the seller, noting all discrepancies that must be corrected and the date by which these corrections must be made. As long as the seller can correct the indicated discrepancies and re-tender the associated items by the buyer's due date, it will be considered to still be in compliance with the contract. However, if the result is a late delivery, then the seller may be subject to damages claims by the buyer, and may no longer qualify for incentive payments.

> **Tip:** The buyer should generally reject any seller suggestions to install defective items, which the seller will then fix. Doing so places excessive reliance on the seller to make the required corrections, which may be delayed or never happen at all. At a minimum, withhold all remaining payments until the corrections have been made.

When items are found to be non-conforming, the buyer can ask the seller for a remediation plan. It can be useful to review the seller's proposed corrective actions in advance, to ensure that they will not result in any modifications that the buyer will find unacceptable.

> **Note:** Any defects not found during the acceptance inspection may still be fixed by the seller at a later date if the contract contains an adequate warranty provision.

A truly serious case of non-conformance may be considered a breach of contract, in which case the buyer may seek to recover payments already made to the seller, and will certainly halt any remaining payments. This situation usually arises when the contract states that time is of the essence in the delivery of the indicated items. When a contract does not state that time is of the essence, then the seller still has a reasonable amount of time in which to perform, even if doing so is after the date specified in the contract. Alternatively, if the seller has tendered a seriously non-conforming item, then the buyer can hold the seller in breach of contract right away, on the grounds that the seller will not be able to cure its performance.

Any rejected items must be prominently labeled as such by the buyer and set aside in a segregated area, so that they are not inadvertently used. This can include storage in a locked area, to eliminate the risk of accidental usage.

> **Tip:** When a non-conformance is found, analyze how the problem occurred and why it was not caught prior to the tender stage. This investigation can result in corrective process changes.

The inspection requirements associated with a tender can be substantial, especially for a large project. This means that the buyer has an obligation to maintain a large and well-qualified inspection staff that can promptly deal with all tenders. This is especially important when the seller has a variety of sub-modules of work that are tendered over the course of a project, such as a series of software modules that are part of a larger system.

Assurance of Performance

Both parties to a contract are working under the assumption that the other party is performing in accordance with the contract terms. If either party has reasonable grounds to suspect that the other party will not be able to perform, it can demand an adequate assurance of performance in writing. Until it receives such assurance, the party making the demand can suspend its contractual activities.

EXAMPLE

A buyer contracts to purchase several air conditioning units from a well-known local manufacturer, with delivery scheduled for May 1. On April 15, the buyer learns that a water main ruptured next to the manufacturer's facility, flooding it. The buyer immediately issues a demand for adequate assurance of performance, which the manufacturer is not able to provide. Accordingly, the buyer treats the contract as having been repudiated.

Final Acceptance

Final acceptance occurs when the buyer accepted all activities required under the terms of a contract. This is typically the end result of a series of inspections of tenders by the seller. At this point, the buyer's project team will turn over the end result to the ultimate user, which is likely to be a team operating in one of the functional areas of the business. For example, the warehouse department might take over a warehouse management system (WMS) for which the programming was overseen by a project team from the IT department. In this example, the warehouse department may conduct its own final inspection before accepting the WMS. Warehouse personnel may also adjust the department's policies and procedures to incorporate the new system into its operations.

A key part of final acceptance is that all documentation is completed. This is needed to ensure that operations manuals fully reflect how an item functions, and that all error conditions and corrections have been properly described for those who will operate it. Depending on the size and complexity of the goods or services being delivered, the completion of all required documentation can be a substantial effort.

Tip: It is generally more cost-effective for the buyer's staff to update any drawings relating to a project that have been marked up by the seller during a construction project, since the buyer will already have the originals stored on its own design software.

Once all final acceptance activities have been completed, the buyer and seller can mutually determine the amount of any incentives owed to the seller, as well as any back charges and liquidated damages to be deducted, resulting in a final payment.

Summary

The contract manager must ensure that the buyer is properly staffed with enough trained people to conduct all final inspections. This is a particular concern when different inspectors are to be used for these inspections than were employed on ongoing project inspections, since there may not be enough people to do so. Also, these inspections are the buyer's last chance to ensure that all items tendered are in conformance with the project specifications; therefore, the contract manager should be willing to play hardball, rejecting non-conforming items and threatening no further payments until all non-conformances have been fixed.

Chapter 8
Demobilization and Close Out

Introduction

When all contract work has been completed, it is time to engage in the demobilization and contract close out process. This involves having the seller remove its personnel and equipment from all buyer facilities, the acceptance of all deliverables by the buyer, the settlement of all remaining disputes, and settlement of all remaining payments. We discuss these topics in the following pages.

Demobilization

Depending on the project type, it may be necessary for the seller and buyer to demobilize, which involves the removal of all personnel and equipment, as well as general clean up of the work site. These topics are addressed further in the following subsections.

Activities by the Seller

The *demobilization* process involves having the seller remove its personnel, equipment, and materials from the buyer's facility. This does not just happen at the end of a project, but whenever a phase of work is complete. At the end of each phase, the seller will pull all personnel and so forth that are no longer needed on the project, so that their costs are no longer charged to it. This is especially important when the underlying contract is fixed price, where cost reduction is essential to generating a decent profit. In the case of a cost reimbursement arrangement, it is the buyer who is more interested in prompt demobilization, to ensure that the costs it reimburses are kept to a minimum.

It can be useful for the contract manager to review a seller's demobilization plan to see if enough qualified personnel will be kept on site to complete all remaining aspects of the job. If this is not the case, the remaining work on the project may drag out past the original due date, simply because there are not enough people on site to complete the work. This is a particular concern when the seller's productivity levels have been low, indicating that more people will be needed to complete the remaining work.

In the case of a cost-reimbursement contract, the buyer will probably have paid for all the materials used for a project. If so, the buyer is entitled to all materials that are still unused at the end of the project. This calls for the formal transfer of materials into the buyer's inventory records. Alternatively, the seller may elect to purchase these materials from the buyer.

It is possible that the buyer loaned some equipment or tools to the seller as part of a project. If so, part of the demobilization process should be a procedure for returning these items to the buyer, as well as reviewing their condition when returned. The result may be a back charge to the seller, if these items are not returned or they are returned in damaged condition. Or, if the buyer had rented equipment for the use of the seller, then it is the seller's responsibility to clean up and return this equipment to the equipment rental company.

If the seller's personnel have been issued security clearances as part of their work within the buyer's facility, then part of the demobilization process will be the return of their passes, as well as the deactivation of their passwords and access codes.

When there is an on-site project, the seller may have constructed temporary facilities to be used by its work teams. These facilities will need to be torn down and removed as part of the demobilization process. Depending on the situation, it may also be necessary for the seller to engage in site restoration work, to return the property to its original condition.

Activities by the Buyer

The buyer will also need to engage in some demobilization at the end of a project. It will likely need to disband the project team, either by shifting them to other projects or returning them to their normal full-time jobs. When the buyer is routinely engaged in similar projects, it may be cost-effective to maintain a permanent project team, in which case the team members will be reassigned to other projects. In particular, the buyer should concentrate on retaining its contract managers, since the most capable ones can greatly reduce the cost of a contract through proper oversight activities.

When the buyer has brought contractors on board to assist with a project, it will likely end these consulting arrangements as soon as the project has ended, given their high cost. However, it can make more sense to retain these people until every possible issue has been resolved that pertains to them. Otherwise, once they are gone, the buyer will not have the expertise on site to deal with any remaining issues, which could unexpectedly increase costs right at the end of a project.

Contract Close Out

A contract must be properly closed out, or else the buyer may have to address a number of lingering concerns that should have been settled during the close out process. Close out activities include the following items:

1. *Verify that all obligations are fulfilled.* Work through the list of all actions that the seller was contractually obligated to complete, and ensure that these actions were taken. A common failing is to not ensure that the final round of inspections and failure corrections were completed.
2. *Complete the final acceptance test.* A final acceptance test should be conducted, verifying that all equipment and other installed systems operate as promised by the seller.
3. *Conduct training.* The ultimate user of the goods or services provided needs to be properly trained in how to use these items, especially if improper use will void the seller's warranty. This includes the completion of any related operating procedures manuals.

4. *Obtain contact information.* If there is a warranty associated with the delivered item, the buyer should obtain contact information from the seller and make it generally available to users, so that they can contact the correct party at the seller in the event of an issue rising.

5. *Clear outstanding liens.* If there are any liens outstanding on buyer property as a result of the contract, work with the seller to clear them. Final payment should not be made until all liens have been cleared.

6. *Settle insurance claims.* Ascertain whether there are any insurance claims associated with the project, and work with the insurer to settle them.

7. *Obtain a release agreement.* This document releases the buyer from any further liabilities that the seller might bring up at a later date, and vice versa. This can be useful when there is a possibility of some residual liabilities causing ongoing negotiations or litigation for an extended period of time.

8. *Settle the accounts.* The contract manager needs to calculate the amount of the final payment due to the seller, which takes into consideration any change orders, incentive payments, back charges, liquidated damages, and so forth.

9. *Rate the seller.* The contract management team assembles a rating of the seller, which can be useful if the buyer ever decides to use it again. This rating should address such matters as whether the work was completed in a timely manner, whether the seller provided a sufficient number of qualified personnel, whether subcontractors were managed properly, the quality level of the completed work, how well it resolved non-conformance issues, and its level of planning and organization.

10. *Conduct a post mortem.* As a final step, the contract manager should conduct a review to see what went well during the project and what did not, so that these issues can be addressed as part of the planning for the next project.

If there are any residual issues between the two parties at the point when final payment is due, it can make sense for the buyer to set aside a portion of the final payment until all issues are settled. Doing so gives it some leverage over the seller in gaining more favorable outcomes. An additional point of leverage for the buyer is that the seller's bonding capacity is reduced for as long as the contract remains open. If the seller happens to be operating at or near the high end of its bonding capacity, then it may be open to a less favorable settlement simply to close the contract and expand its available bonding capacity for other projects.

Document Retention

A normal result of contract management is a great deal of paperwork. Of particular importance is the paperwork associated with change orders and claims made against the seller, since these items are routinely being disputed. Accordingly, the contract manager should maintain files for all documents related to these items, stored by the identifying order or claim number. Besides change orders and claims, the contract manager's team should have compiled a substantial amount of documentation regarding the work, covering such matters as routine meetings with seller personnel, daily logs of activities, and photographs of the work in progress. All of these documents may be needed to settle disputes with the seller, and so should be retained through the period when either party can file a claim.

Tip: When handwritten logs are maintained for a project, use a bound volume to ensure that pages cannot be removed or added. When an electronic log is being used, the system should not allow any log entries to be changed. These actions are needed so that the logs will be seen as credible evidence of the activities during a project.

Besides the documentation generated by the contract manager's team, the seller will also forward such items as operating manuals, quality assurance documentation, warranties, and engineering drawings – all of which must be properly stored. When the buyer's inspection team inspects tendered items, it may collect any quality assurance documentation created by the seller, such as material test reports and process certifications. These documents will also need to be stored.

Given the expense of office space, what is the best way to retain project documentation? There are several issues to consider that can reduce the storage burden. One such issue is the existence of a formal document destruction policy. This policy is designed to ensure that all contract-related documents are retained for a certain period of time, after which their status will be reviewed, and they will be destroyed if no longer needed. Doing so ensures that there is a regular process in place for examining and dispositioning old contracts. For example, there may be a policy that mandates contract destruction 10 years after the termination date of a contract. Whatever policy is implemented, be sure to first consult with legal counsel, to ensure that there are no statutes that will be violated if a contract and associated documents are destroyed too early. The following table notes several types of purchasing documents for which different retention periods might be mandated.

Types of Purchasing Documents

Document Type	Retention Period
Contracts	Legal counsel should make a determination of the most appropriate time period over which contracts should be retained after they have been closed.
Project documentation	Normally maintained by the department that was responsible for the project; retention is based on company policy – there are not usually any legally-mandated retention periods.
Purchase orders	Open purchase orders are always retained; closed purchase orders should be retained for at least six years.
Seller report cards	There is no legal reason to retain report cards, but they should be retained as long as a seller is active, to provide background on historical performance.

Another issue is when to shift contract documentation off-site. Once a contract's termination date has been reached, it may still make sense to keep it on-site if there is a successor contract, as there may be a need to consult the arrangement in the prior contract. However, once any pressing need for on-site contract retention has passed, one should shift it to a secure off-site storage area and enter its storage location in an index, so that it can be readily located if needed.

A variation on the off-site storage concept is to purchase contract management software, and enter the essential elements of each contract into the software. By doing so, the original document can be immediately shifted off-site. In addition, the information in each contract is now accessible to anyone having access to the software, so it can be reviewed in multiple locations at the same time.

Summary

When conducting the demobilization and close out processes, consider doing so from a standard checklist. This is useful when the number of these activities is substantial, and there is a risk that some of the items might otherwise be missed. Therefore, checklists are an essential element of the process for larger projects, while a reduced checklist might be more appropriate for smaller projects.

Chapter 9
Warranties and Remedies

Introduction

A *warranty* is a guarantee related to the performance of assets that are owned by the party being guaranteed. A guarantee is frequently required in connection with the sale of goods or services to the party being guaranteed. If the warranty is related to a product, the seller normally replaces or repairs the product in question. If the warranty is related to a service, the seller usually provides a full or partial refund, or replacement services. In this chapter, we discuss warranties and other remedies that may be available to a buyer.

Express Warranties

An *express warranty* is an agreement by a seller to provide repairs or a replacement for a faulty product within a specified period of time after it was purchased. The warranty can be worded in a variety of ways. For example, it might state, "We guarantee all of our shed products against defects in construction for one year. When a structural defect is brought to our attention, we will repair or replace it."

An express warranty can be included in the seller's contract, but may also be contained within a statement on an advertisement, in a catalog, or in a sign in a store. It is not necessary for a warranty statement to even include the words "warranty" or "guarantee" in order to create an express warranty.

A seller creates an express warranty when it indicates that all goods sold will conform to its statements about the performance of the goods. For example, "this computer keyboard will last for 10 million keystrokes" is an express warranty. An express warranty can also relate to the description of the goods being sold. For example, "Wisconsin cheese" represents a warranty that the cheese being sold originated in Wisconsin.

A buyer can recover from a breach of an express warranty if the warranty statement helped to persuade the buyer to purchase a product. The amount that can be recovered equals the difference between the value of the goods with the associated warranty, and the actual value of the goods purchased.

EXAMPLE

A seller of used business jets warrants that a used eight-seat jet has been flown only 500,000 miles. If this statement is true, then the jet is worth $3.2 million. However, the jet was actually flown six times more miles, which reduces its value to $1.8 million. A buyer purchases the jet for $3 million, then discovers the excessive flight time, and sues the seller for damages. The amount of the damages that can be recovered is $1.4 million, which is calculated as the difference between the warranted value and the actual value. The $3 million price paid is irrelevant to this calculation.

A common misunderstanding between buyers and sellers is whether the standard salesman chatter associated with a sale is part of the seller's express warranty. This chatter is merely a statement of opinion, and so is not part of the seller's express warranty. The difference between salesperson chatter and a warranty statement is whether a reasonable buyer would find the salesperson's statement to be reliable.

EXAMPLE

The seller of a custom-designed camper van states that "you will sleep better in this than you would believe possible." This is only an opinion, and so is not an express warranty. However, if the seller says "this camper van gets 20 miles per gallon," that is an express warranty, because it is presumed to be a statement of fact.

Note: An express warranty cannot be excluded by a contract clause that disclaims all express or implied warranties, on the grounds that offering an inducement through an express warranty and then withdrawing it would be a violation of good faith.

Implied Warranties

Depending on the circumstances, a warranty can be implied, even when there is no express warranty. These warranties are not stated in a contract. The types of implied warranties are described in the following sub-sections.

Implied Warranty of Fitness for a Particular Purpose

This warranty is applicable when the seller has made statements that the goods being sold meet the specific requirements of the buyer. The warranty is breached in all cases where these statements turn out not to be true. The warranty is applicable when the seller knows about the purpose for which goods are being purchased and then makes a statement that the goods will indeed serve this purpose, and the buyer relies on this statement when making the purchase.

EXAMPLE

Eskimo Construction is a well-known provider of insulated huts for use in arctic conditions. A buyer visits the Eskimo showroom and describes his requirements, which include being able to survive through the winter on an island in extremely northern Canada. The salesperson selects a particular model for the buyer. The selected model turns out to be woefully under-insulated, resulting in the buyer suffering from severe hypothermia. The buyer can sue Eskimo for breach of the implied warranty of fitness for a particular purpose.

Implied Warranty of Merchantability

When the seller is classified as a merchant, then there is an implied warranty of merchantability associated with its sales contracts, unless such a warranty is specifically disclaimed. This implied warranty mandates that the seller meet the following standards:

- The goods are fit for their intended purpose.
- The goods are of a quality that would pass without objection in the trade.
- The goods are of consistent quality.
- The goods are properly packaged and labeled.
- The goods conform to the statements made on the container.
- The goods have at least a mid-range of quality.

EXAMPLE

A workbench must be sufficiently robust to withstand the normal loads usually placed on a workbench.

EXAMPLE

A container that states the contents are skim milk should in fact contain skim milk, and not whole milk.

This type of warranty does not apply when someone not classified as a merchant makes a sale. Thus, the implied warranty of merchantability applies to a merchant who sells a computer to a customer, but not when a neighbor sells a similar computer to another neighbor.

Construction Warranties

In a construction contract, there is an implied warranty that the associated work will be completed in a proper and workmanlike manner. The duty of the contractor includes the quality of the materials used in construction. Given the existence of this implied warranty, the buyer should conduct a final acceptance inspection and issue a written notification to the seller, itemizing all non-conforming items found. The buyer should then withhold the final payment until the issues included in its notification letter have been remediated by the seller.

A construction warranty that protects the seller instead of the buyer covers the adequacy of plans and specifications. In essence, if the plans and specifications provided to the seller by the buyer are inadequate, then the seller is entitled to payment when it has complied with the buyer's plans and specifications, even though the buyer claims that the resulting product is insufficient. This warranty is not voided when a contract clause requires the seller to review the plans and visit the site prior to commencing work. However, if the seller does *not* comply with defective plans and specifications, then the seller must then proceed without the benefit of this warranty.

A potential point of contention is whether an identified construction problem originated from the materials used or seller workmanship, or because the resulting work is not suitable for the purpose specified by the buyer. In the first case, the contractor is responsible for remediating the problem. However, if the specifications supplied by the buyer are faulty, or those specifications are unsuitable for the intended purpose of the project, then this issue is not covered under the seller's warranty.

In cases where the seller recommends a replacement for goods that have been specified by the buyer and the buyer approves this swap, then the buyer is considered to have adopted these items, and therefore assumes the risk of their being unsuitable for their intended purpose. However, the buyer can contractually shift this responsibility over to the seller.

If the seller is involved in the development of specifications for a project, then it can be held liable for the unsuitability of the eventual product, depending on the extent to which it was involved in the development work and its level of knowledge in regard to the specifications. It is also possible that the seller can be held liable if it should know that the specifications or goods are clearly defective, and yet does not notify the buyer that this is the case.

The Warranty Period

A warranty period typically begins when a seller offers to transfer goods to a buyer. In the case of a product installation where the seller is responsible for the installation, the warranty period begins when installation has been completed. In cases where the buyer is responsible for the installation, the warranty period begins when the seller delivers the goods to the buyer's location. However, when the contract states that the goods must be installed and tested to ensure that they are in conformance with the underlying contract, the warranty period does not begin until conformance has been proved.

Tip: During the warranty period, installed equipment may need to be serviced properly or else the warranty will be voided. This means that the user needs to be fully trained in how to operate and maintain the equipment.

Warranty Disclaimers

When a seller makes an express warranty regarding the goods being sold, it can also limit the extent of the warranty. Further, an implied warranty can be disclaimed, though only if the seller follows these rules:

- The seller states that the goods are being sold as is;
- The seller states that there is no implied warranty of merchantability; or
- The seller states that there is no implied warranty of fitness for a particular purpose.

When disclaimers are employed, they must be conspicuously displayed where they would be noticed by a reasonable person. Otherwise, a court will declare the disclaimers to be invalid.

Tip: To make a disclaimer more noticeable, state the relevant language in bold, in a larger font, and/or in a different color from the surrounding text.

Remedies

In order to obtain a remedy from a seller for a breach of warranty, the buyer must issue a notification of breach to the seller within a reasonable period of time. If no such notice is given, then the buyer loses its right to the recovery of damages from the seller. This notification requirement gives the seller extra time to understand the facts underlying a breach, so that it can develop a defense for its position. Thus, any notification delay that prevents the seller from learning the facts would be considered an unreasonable delay.

Most of the remedies available to a buyer were stated in the Monetary Damages sub-section in Chapter 1, where one might pursue compensatory damages, consequential damages, liquidated damages, or tort damages, depending on the situation. When dealing with warranties, the most common remedies are for the seller to either repair or replace the goods in question, or to issue a refund for some or all of the purchase price. At a more expansive level, the seller is responsible for the removal of an asset, its transport to a repair facility, completion of the required repairs, transport back to the buyer, and re-installation of the asset. In cases where the buyer is unable to function as a result of the asset failure, the buyer may also be able to sue for the recovery of lost profits, as well as for damage to other assets caused by the failure.

Another remedy for the buyer when acquired goods fail is to obtain replacements and then charge the seller for the cost of the replacements, along with all associated transport and installation costs. In this case, the buyer has a duty to minimize the cost of the replacements, thereby curtailing the warranty costs of the seller. If a buyer does not minimize replacement costs, it may find that a court will not award it the full amount of the costs incurred.

Summary

The law regarding warranties varies by jurisdiction, so the first step for the parties involved in a breach of warranty claim is to research which laws apply to the specific circumstances. This information can then be used by both parties to derive a strategy for how to pursue and defend against a warranty claim. Once a buyer has developed a history of dealing with similar claims, it can adjust the terms and conditions of its contracts to afford it maximum protection; conversely, a seller's experience with these claims will influence its own contractual approach to warranties.

Glossary

A

Accord. When the parties to a contract agree to a compromise solution.

Assignment of rights. When a party to a contract transfers its contractual rights to other parties.

B

Back charge. A demand by a buyer for compensation to offset costs incurred to perform work that the seller should have performed.

C

Change order. A document that is used to record an amendment to the original contract.

Claim. A seller notification, stating that it has found a condition not covered by the contract scope, or which interferes with its work.

Competitive bidding. When a number of sellers bid against each other, presumably resulting in the lowest possible price.

Consideration. Something of legal value that is given in exchange for a promise.

Contract. An agreement between two parties that creates mutual legal obligations.

Contracting risk. An uncertainty that, if it were to occur, would adversely impact the contracting objectives.

Covenant. An absolute promise to perform.

Critical path. The longest path in a project plan.

D

Demobilization. A process that involves having the seller remove its personnel, equipment, and materials from the buyer's facility.

E

Exculpatory clause. A contract provision that relieves one party of liability if damages occur during the execution of a contract.

Executory contract. A contract that has not yet been fully performed or fully executed.

Express warranty. An agreement by a seller to provide repairs or a replacement for a faulty product within a specified period of time after it was purchased.

F

Fraud. A false misrepresentation of the facts, resulting in the object of the fraud receiving an injury by acting upon the misrepresented facts.

I

Inferior performance. When the actions of a party impairs or destroys the essence of a contract.

Injunction. A court order requiring a person to do or stop doing a specific action.

N

Novation. When a third party takes the place of one of the original parties to a contract.

P

Personal satisfaction test. When the person given the right to reject services does so in good faith.

Promissory estoppel. The legal principle that a contract is enforceable, even if made without formal consideration when the offeror has made a promise to an offeree, who then relies on that promise to his or her subsequent detriment.

R

Reasonable person test. When performance by a reasonable person constitutes acceptance of performance.

Request for proposal. A business document that announces a project, describes it, and solicits bids from qualified sellers to complete it.

Restraint of trade. Any activity that prevents another party from conducting business as they normally would.

Reverse auction. When a buyer puts up a request for a required good or service, and sellers place bids for the amount they are willing to be paid; at the end of the auction, the seller with the lowest bid wins.

S

Satisfaction. When parties complete their performance under the terms of an accord.

Sole source. When only one supplier, to the best of the buyer's knowledge, is capable of delivering a required product or service.

Strict performance. When all of the terms stipulated in a contract have been met.

Substantial performance. When there is a minor breach of the terms of a contract.

T

Table of conformance. A listing of every requirement set forth by a buyer, with a notation next to it regarding whether the bidder's offering will meet the requirement.

Tender. When a seller is ready to deliver completed goods or services to the buyer in accordance with the contract requirements.

U

Unconscionable contract. A contract that is so one-sided that it is unfair to one party and is therefore unenforceable under the law.

Uniform Commercial Code. The body of laws governing commercial transactions in the United States.

W

Warranty. A guarantee related to the performance of assets that are owned by the party being guaranteed.

Index

www.ingramcontent.com/pod-product-compliance
Lightning Source LLC
Chambersburg PA
CBHW081509200326
41518CB00015B/2442